He Is MY MOTHER'S FATHER

By

Anwar Al-Haqq

I was a 12th grade student. Make the long story short. One evening I saw two of my cousins were at our grandparents' room with them. My grandpa's eyes were over the newspaper. My cousins were competing with each other who would tell their story first to grandma. Finally grandma decided she who would tell first their story about soccer game. My cousins were very eager to tell their skill about their soccer game to grandma. They also found grandma as their listener. My grandma was listening their soccer skill. She was impressed to listen their story. One my cousin told "I was running with the ball and two of the opposite side players were in front of me to tackle me. But I run with the ball and kick the ball and

He Is My Mother's Father -- ☺ Anwar Al-Haqq

score a goal." They also acted to show my grandma how they did it. Grandpa's eyes were over the newspaper and asked softly "is that right?" I gave a look to grandpa. Grandma also gave a look at grandpa with smile and gave a nod which mean "yes her grandchild did it". Other cousin told "one of our player gave a corner kick and I jump up to head the ball and score a goal." Grandpa asked again softly "is that right?" I was watching their activities with patient and I told grandpa nicely "if you don't want to read the newspaper, please let me to read it." He became mad to me. Sometime I think "what I should do with this mad person". This mad person's daughter who is my mother always remind me that I have to behave well with her parents which I am listening since I learned to understand the language. It is sound to me that her parents are like a magician. If I behave well, all the good things would happen in my life. If I just hurt their feeling, all the bad thing would happen in my life because her parents has special communication with God. In my mind "I just have to hurt their feeling and all the magical things would happen and I would see me in misery." Because of it even I think that what they are doing is odd to me but I have to living with them by showing my tolerance and not to advise them to do something which is meaningful in life and also smart. I found always to live with them by modify my desire or I have to compromise my desire. As I could remember that when I was a child, my grandpa considered that he should sometime need to entertain me. But he was not a comedian who can act or say something that could made me to laugh. All he could do is to tickling on my tummy which made me to laugh. It was a one of my childhood life when my grandpa felt to entertain me. He was ticking in my tummy. I used my lower extremities to protect my tummy. I brought my knees close to my chest but side of the abdomen did not cover by my lower extremity. Now grandpa started tickling on my left or right tummy. I was curving left to right and right to left and I was laughing loudly. The success for the attempt to make me to laugh loudly bring the smile to the face of my grandpa. My mom came to the room after a while and saw the activity of the grandpa. She also was looking at my situation and I was trying to guarding my tummy from the grandpa's funny fingers. My mom also smiling. Today I think if I would do the same things to her father, she would think I violate the right of her father and she would be mad to me. Well! my cousins were 2nd grade student at that time and my grandma were not present at the soccer field when two of my cousins were playing soccer. But she was pretending that she was at the field to watch their game. Anyway this me. I am a Rontu. I just came from Bangladesh after I visited my family there. It was constantly coming in my mind some of the incident happen in Bangladesh. I am a second year Engineering student in an American University.

That's My Family

He Is My Mother's Father -- ☺   Anwar Al-Haqq

It was a cold but sunny day of January in St. Louis, Missouri. It was Saturday. Friday Rontu came from Bangladesh. The memory of his family was coming in his mind what he left behind in Bangladesh to study Engineering in the USA. He was quietly sitting in his reading table. He took a note book and started writing.

Rontu wrote about his trip to Bangladesh "I was walking in the Forest Park, St. Louis, Missouri at 2 o'clock."   And he continued "It was month of December and was very cold. My fall semester was over. I was feeling thrill to go to Bangladesh. While I was walking in the park, I felt so excited to go to Bangladesh. Yes I am going to visit my family in Bangladesh. Tomorrow. One and a half years I missed my parents and my only brother and sister, my grandparents, my aunt and uncle and their children. My mother is the first child of my grandpa. My uncle and my aunt are the second and third child of my grandpa respectably. My brother has a three years old daughter. Like my father, my brother, my sister-in-law are a medical doctor. We were known as a doctor family in our Town. My sister is the 4th year's medical student. And I heard my sister has a fiancé who is doing his medical training. I am the youngest among my sibling and was sent to study engineering in the USA by my parents. My mother is a professor in English in a college. My uncle and his wife are a medical doctor and have two sons and one daughter. Oldest son was preparing to take the 12th grade final exam. He was studying hard to get admission in the medical school. Daughter and younger son are in the 9th and 4th grade respectively. My aunt is a medical doctor and her husband is an Engineer. They have a son and a daughter. Son is in 4th grade and daughter is in 1st grade student. They are my mother's sibling. My father was the only child and paternal grandparents decease long ago. My dad did not talk about his father with us. I just know from my mother and uncle of my father that my paternal grandpa was a teacher in an Islamic School. He had the equivalent 12 grade level of education in the Islamic religious study. My paternal grandma was a homemaker. My parents, my siblings, my aunt and my uncle and their family live in a same building which own by my maternal grandpa. My grandpa is 70 years old." I was a 12th grade student.

Last one and half years I sometime called in Bangladesh. I talked

He Is My Mother's Father -- ☺ Anwar Al-Haqq

with everyone. Most of the time, my mother called me from Bangladesh. In our conversation she was more interested to tell how her granddaughter was keeping her busy and how naughty she was. One day my mom told me that she was coming from the living room. My niece was with my sister-in-law. They were playing. When my sister-in-law saw my mother she said with smile and with rebuff to my niece "hold on there". My niece runs to my mother. "Grandma she is going to kill me" my niece told while run to my mother. My mother little rush to rescue her little granddaughter and hold her granddaughter between her arms. My mother gave her a big hug. My mother said "how it would be like if someone would kill you." Just after that, my niece turned to her mother and said "did you able to catch me?" My sister-in-law smile and went to her room. My mother sat at a chair. My niece was on her lap and holding her firmly on hers arms. "You think if you be with me no one will able to tell or do anything against you". I am giving another incident of when my sister-in-law is with my niece and when she just sees my mother how she becomes harsh to my niece. One day my sister-in-law's parents and her uncles, aunts from both of her mother's and father side came to visit her. 16 of them. My mother was at college. My father took them to show a building recently built. Still construction was going. My mother came from college. My sister-in-law looked at my mother and understood that she was not tired or in bad mood. My niece were playing and making little noise at the corridor. My sister-in-law went to my niece and talked loudly to rebuff her "playing and playing whole day. Did I not tell you not making any noise here? Did I? You are not listening to me." After rebuff my niece, she left. My niece became upset. She looked very sad. My mother went to my niece and took her to the living room. My mother sat in a chair and her granddaughter was in her lap. My niece looked very sad. My mother tried be bring her good mood back. My mother was talking and my niece was listening but was not saying anything. My father and 16 of his guests entered the living room. My dad saw her granddaughter was in bad mood.
"what happened to her?" my father asked.
"mom scolded." my mother said with little sadly but was smile in her face. My niece sad face also entertains my parents.
"She did nothing" my mother added after a pause.
"why need to scold her when she did nothing" my father said softly to support his granddaughter. Everyone support my father and also support my niece and sat at the living room.

He Is My Mother's Father -- ☺   Anwar Al-Haqq

"come to me" my father said to my niece."
go to your grandpa" my mother said to my niece.
My niece stood up sadly from the lap of my mother and sadly walked to my father. My mother was watching her with smile when she was walking toward my father. My father let her in sit in his lap. "my good granddaughter" My father said. My father was talking and she was listening. First she was just listening. After a while she gradually responds to my dad. And her mood went up. After a while my dad said to my niece "Allah! Let see can you smile?" My niece smiled with my dad. "go and bring the newspaper for me from my room" my dad asked my niece. My niece took off the lap of my dad and walked away from our living room to the bed room of my parents. My mom was still talking with the guests.

At night my niece fell in sleep at the bed of my parents. My sister-in-law carried her to their bed room and put her on the bed. My brother was sitting at the room and was reading a book. He stood up to help my sister-in-law to make a bed for my niece. "I did not find anyone to talk on behalf of me. Her all grandparents took on her side." my sister-in-law was talking herself when she put my niece in her bed.
"you are messing around with someone when all her grandparents are ready to support her. If her grandpa was a Primary school teacher, he would tell you to grab your own ears and sit down and stand up for at least 10 times as a punishment to scold his granddaughter for nothing" my brother said. My sister-in-law smile but show little anger to hear the words of my brother. My brother gave her a hug. "well! if my father-in-law would tell me to do so, I would not have any option except to do it" my sister-in-law said. This story of my family reminds me the school system in Bangladesh and how the school teacher disciplines the students. This is one the way our school teacher punish the students. Students have to grab their ears and sit down and stand up considered as to give some kind of shame who did not do the home work and also did not study. Caning is most popular to most teachers. Every school at their office keeps cane to punish the student. Some teacher invents how to physically torture the student. Most of the teacher most of the time interested to torture the students then to teach the students. Sometime the teacher spend 40 minute out of 50 minutes to torture the students. One class hours is 50 minutes. And they taught nothing to the students. I found the

goal for the teacher to teach the student get less important than their goal to torture the students. And this punishment system discourage the students come to the class. I did not find any effectiveness to torture the students and able to teach the students. But our culture was built up with the norm that torture could help a person to be human enough and also could help to learn. When the parents hire a private tutor, some of them tell the teacher "bone is for me and the skin, flesh and the soft tissue are for the teacher." They give the private tutor to let their son and daughter to be torture over their skin so that they could feel the pain. Some tutor and the school teacher punish hard that it also penetrate the bone. After punished the students, they said "the place hit by his or her cane that will go to the heaven". But I did not find such claim authentic in my religion. Most of the religious school teachers are very harsh compare to the general education school. Why the religious teacher punished their students most of the time, I did not get the answer. And often they are rude to the students. But our prophet (SAW) was best teacher and he treated people nicely. How come these religious teachers could claim them that they are following our prophet when they are unnecessary harsh to their students? Because the religious teachers are very harsh to the student, most of the time they discourage the student to come to learn the religion. These students are often under 10 years old. Probably the religious teacher found them as a weak person and subject to be torture.

One day I went with my grandpa to one of our neighbor. A private tutor was teaching two of his students. He was caning them and they were crying. I do not know how they are leaning when they were living in panic. My grandpa said without letting the teacher to know "it barbaric. Any teacher would torture his or her students should be fire". I gave support my grandpa instantly. I did not take time to think to support my grandpa. Compare to his time, situation of torturing the students getting little better. School teacher are getting little civilized then before. As young and week the students are, they are more vulnerable to be torture. Like the primary school students are more vulnerable to be torture (on the contrary, University professors are worried to be torture by their students). Also has the discrimination of the poor and rich. One of my teachers who torture the students said "after fight with the wife and become frustrated, how can I teach you all". He dumped all his frustration to

He Is My Mother's Father -- ☺ Anwar Al-Haqq

the students. And the whole administration did not come to intervene this frustrated man to stop to torture the students, but they encourage them. I saw the little power they have how they are abusing it in the name of teaching the students. I was trying to remember my grandpa's time. He was a son of the Chairman. Did he able to escape the punishment? It was not sound like that. But I saw my parents, my brother and my sister-in-law teach my niece when she was in their lap. And they talked with her. They play with her and teach her. She can tell all the alphabet of Bengali, English and Arabic. She can recite the 4 small chapters from the Koran, 4/5 Bengali poems. But the caning system in school did not get my support, if they sincerely want to teach students. I even heard that some teachers don't know what to teach, so they took the scaring tactic. And they torture the students.

Yes I am going to my country where a lot of systems and idea are proven to be nonfunctional but people still practicing it. Even all these nonfunctional things exist in my society, still I love my country where my family live and I would be with them after one and a half years. That made me to feel joys.

Some of the past incident was constantly coming in my mind. I indulged them to come in my mind this time. During the semester a lot of time I was struggling to block those memories that they could not come in my mind and prevent me to concentrate in my studying. One and half years ago, I just got the student Visa to come to the USA to study. Jolly became curious to know more about the USA then before. She learned that most of the American has a car and they drive their own car. At that time she was a seven grade student. One day my grandpa was reading the newspaper at the living room and my grandma was woven woolen cloth. Jolly came to the living room and sat next to grandpa and read the newspaper for a while. Then he whisper to grandma "let bother grandma".

Grandpa pretended that he did not hear anything.

"grandpa do you know that most of the American has a car and they drive their own car" Jolly added after remain silent for a while and was planning how could she bother grandma.

"yes I heard of it" grandpa respond.

"grandpa! Do you know that some of the highway, people could drive the car 100 miles an hours" Jolly said.

"I know" grandpa said.

Grandma was sitting another Sofa where 3 people can sit easily.

He Is My Mother's Father -- ☺ Anwar Al-Haqq

Jolly went and sit next to grandma. She took a stick and made it as steering of the car. She moved it around like she was moving the steering of the car.

"everyone need to fasten the sit belt" Jolly said.

Grandma pretended that she did not hear anything. Jolly started at grandma with frown face for a while. Grandma ignore her and shown that she was busy to woven the woolen cloth. After a while, Jolly said again "everyone needs to fasten the sit belt".

Still grandma did not pay attention to Jolly. Jolly stared at grandma with the frown face again.

"O, Ma! She does not want to listen anyone. How stubborn a person could be? " Jolly talked with herself with surprise.

Grandma still did not pay attention to Jolly. She was woven the woolen cloth. Grandpa was smiling behind the newspaper. Jolly moved little over grandma to show that she was helping grandma to fasten the sit belt. Jolly shown that she pulled the sit belt and made sound that she fasten the sit belt for grandma. Jolly took the stick which she would use to show a steering of the car. She started to made sound with her mouth that she was driving a car.

"the speed of the car is now 100 miles an hours" Jolly said.

"how can you drive a car 100 miles an hours where 65 miles is the speed limit?" grandma asked her with rebuff.

"slow down your car" grandma rebuff her again while woven the woolen cloth.

Jolly stared at grandma with frown face.

"look straight ahead. How could someone drive a car when she was looking at the side of the car?" grandma said with surprise.

"do you want to make an accident?" grandma said with rebuff.

Jolly pretend that she was driving a car and it was making sound.

"slow down your car. Speed of the car is still high. Slow it down." grandma said with rebuff.

"stop the car" grandma said with rebuff after a while.

"it is danger sit in your car" Grandma added.

Jolly shown that she made a hard brake and stop the car.

"if you break hard like this, no one would be at the car. They will be outside the car. Where did you learn to drive a car?" grandma said rebuff.

"I did not start the car yet." Jolly said softly to grandma.

"how did you drive a car without stared the car?" grandma rebuff her again.

"it would hard to drive a car while she would be at the passenger

sit" Jolly said with little somberly.
"I would not give her a ride" Jolly added.
Jolly stood up from the sofa and went to grandpa and sat next to him.
"you would understand who she is" grandpa said to Jolly.
Jolly took few pages of the newspaper and started reading it.

My grandpa often said "let kids not always make a subject of to be discipline. Let them also to grown by assisting them to think to make their own decision under the supervision of the older people. And let them also to choose what game they become more interested to play as long as it would not harm other. If kids just remain under the control, they could always look at other to make decision for them in their whole life." I saw grandpa most the time did not control us and did not choose for us what we should do. His statement was "Let the kids the freedom to grown until their growth will not harm other even they do the silly things in their life. From the silly thing just help them to think wisely and help them to come out from doing the silly things". I saw he is the man what he believed that he also put in action.

Three years ago, I saw grandma was yelling to everyone at the balcony. Grandpa was sitting at the balcony and was reading the newspaper. She was mad. She seemed to mad to everyone.
"no one wants to listen to me" grandma said loudly.
It did not bother grandpa that much. Most of the time grandpa made her mad. But some mysterious reason sometime she just yell to everyone but don't mention grandpa's name. And all her children rush to take care of her. They wanted to know what her problem was. They probably already know that there was not any serious problem involve that cause her to be mad. That day was one those days to show the madness of our grandma. Her grandchildren came to the balcony out of curiosity. They did not take it seriously. My brother came and sat next to grandpa.
"she probably just did it to get the attention" my brother said in whispered voice to grandpa.
Grandpa looked at to my brother with little disapproval.
"I said 'probably'" my brother added.
Grandpa pretended that he did not gave much attention to my brother. But if I said grandpa that day "grandma did it to get the attention", it could made him annoyed and very annoyed for sure.

He Is My Mother's Father --☺   Anwar Al-Haqq

"how long a person can just stay inside a building" grandma said. All her children show that whatever she said she was right. Grandma's son did not know what to do. He was readily accepted to meet grandma's demand. My mother was the leading person to cool down grandma. So whatever my mother was saying, grandma's son readily supports it. Sometime grandma's younger daughter also took the lead to cool her down.
"that's right" my uncle said to meet the demand of grandma.
"what do you do all the time? Can you take your grandma at the park? Your grandma could walk at the fresh air of the park" my uncle told with rebuff to his son Azam.

Azam was listening to his father. He already know that my uncle just rebuff him to give the consolation to our grandma. Azam behave that It was his fault. This was probably grandma's weekly or semi-monthly or monthly routine for yelling to everyone. But poor Azam was to blame for everything. Azam is paying the cost to be an obedient child of the family.
"this evening I would take grandma to the Park" Azam said politely.

Lilly looked at grandma. She took her tongue out from her mouth and show to grandma with grimacing face. Grandma saw it. She just stared at her for a while without showing any reacting. She turn out her face away from Lilly. She was mad to the previous matter. She did not say anything to her. It did not bother her. My aunt saw that Lilly show her grimacing faces to grandma.
"what are you doing here? Go to your father" my aunt rebuff Lilly. Lilly went to their room.
"if I would take my tongue out and show my grimacing face to your grandma, she would take whole house over her head by yelling to everyone." grandpa told softly to my brother that only he could hear what our grandpa said to him.
My brother tried to convince grandpa why our grandma would not yelling to Lilly.
"Lilly is just a child and child are considered always an innocent person. Whatever they do still it is considered as an innocent act". my brother said to grandpa.
"by the wish of God, you have sense. And you also has intelligent and wisdom. How would it be like if an intelligent person like you would behave like an innocent girl? It would automatically make anyone mad. Particularly our grandma." my bother added.

My grandpa concentrated to read the newspaper. And all I saw the struggle of the children of my grandma not to let their heaven to be displace underneath of their mother's feet. As our prophet (SAW) said "heaven of the children are underneath the feet of their mother." They are also following the teaching of our prophet.

Coming Back To Bangladesh

Day before I would go to Bangladesh, I met with Jania and her two years old grandson at the Park. Jania came from Ukraine and we some time practice English at the library. I just go to this class to meet with some new people and looking for the opportunity to talk about the religion and also to know the culture of these people. Before I met with Jania, I saw Jania's grandson was running away from her at the park. She was running behind to catch him. But her grandson was far ahead of her. I asked "do you want me to catch him?" Jania node for approval. I run very fast like to running to win 100 meter race and crossed the boy without catching him. After crossed the boy about 30 yards, I stop and turned back and bowed down with my hands which were supported over my knees. I raised my right hand and gave the direction to the boy to go back to his grandma. But the boy ran to give me a hug. I hold him as long Jenia did not come close to us. Jenia was talking herself by nodding to her grandson "as you are growing older, it is getting difficult for me to manage you." I put him in the ground and Jania hold his hand. "How are you?" Jenia asked me.
"Not bad." I said.
"When are you going to Bangladesh?"
"Tomorrow, 5 O'clock in the evening."
"Excited!"
"Off course! Clock is becoming lazy now a day. Are you going to the library today?" I asked Jenia.
"Yes" she said."
"I will see you at the Library at 7 O'clock. Mrs. Carroll would be today." Carroll is the English teacher.
"I know" Jenia respond.
"I need to go to buy a toy for my niece. Bye!
Bye."

7 O'clock I was at the Public library. I saw Jenia, Carroll and two

He Is My Mother's Father -- ☺   Anwar Al-Haqq

other new students were sitting in the library. I went to them and sat next to Carroll. We introduce ourselves to each other and we told each other where we all were come from. I was little excited. I am going home. But tried to suppress my felling that people would not ask each other "does he have an Euphoria? Does he has any Bipolar type mental problem?" This was an English conversation class. Our Topic was about the Global Warming. Carroll brought the topic because Al Gore got the noble prize for it.
"It was a mistake to give Al Gore the noble prize for the Global Warming. There is nothing exists like Global warming" I said.
"There is a Global warming" Carroll reply with confidence.
"It's very cold today does not mean that Global warming does not exit." she added.
"There is a global warming" Jania told to support Carroll.
Everyone agrees with Carroll that there is a global warming. I looked at Jania. She was not confidence about her English speaking. She thought she could have mistake to speak a correct English sentence.
"I need to translate word to word from the Ukrainian language to English" Jania said.
""If she translated word to word and said "Ground the playground. Whatever it is in Ukraine language"" I said and look at Carroll.
"I don't know" Carroll responded and tried to be a naïve person.
Jania said "I don't ground the playground. I took my grandson to the playground".

I was very excited to go home. Sometime I felt that I was over excited. I was not behaving normally to the people that day at the English conversation class. Our English Conversation class was 7 to 8 in the evening. After the class, I returned to my apartment and tried to sleep earlier. But hardly I was able to sleep 3 hours. Most of the time, I just Lie down in my bed. Constantly thoughts were coming in my head of my parents, sibling, my grandparents, my aunt and my uncle and their family. I live in the USA and I am no longer a kid. My opinion should be heard. My sister probably would show some kind of respect and let other to listen my opinion. All my life I have to listen and she need to talk. Sometime I tried to block those thoughts which were constantly coming in my head. And I was thinking how everyone would receive me at the Airport. My mother still considers me as her baby. These random thought were constantly coming in my head.

Next day I wake up earlier and Packed my luggage and arrived at the airport two hours before the plan would depart from the airport.

After 26 hours of the plane journey, I arrived at the Dhaka International Airport, Dhaka. It was 15 th of December. I saw my parents, my grandparents and my siblings, my cousins were waiting for me at the airport. I received a warm welcome from them. My grandparents were happy to see me like the other members of my family.

Introducing Bangladesh

In 1958, over 90% of the Bangladeshi people used to live in the rural area. It was a province of Pakistan at that time. That time Bangladesh was considered as East Pakistan. The form of Government was like that: home. Few homes to create the house; houses to create a village, villages to create a Union; Union to created Station; Station to create the District; districts to created Sub-division; sub-division to create the province; Provinces to create the Country. After Bangladesh got independent from Pakistan, sub-division created the country. Bangladesh has no province. Local Government started from the Union which they called Union Parishad. A chairman is elected by the people. And also each village elects the Member for the Union Parishad. At City, people elect the Mayor. And city divided into the Ward. And every ward also has a ward commissioner.

Bangladesh, a country located in the South-East Asia. Also some people called it the Indian subcontinent. Before the British, it was rule by a Muslim rulers. The last Muslim ruler name was Nabab Siraj-ud-Daulla. He was the king for the Bengal (included west Bengal in India), Bihar and Orissa in India. British rule India subcontinent for 200 hundred years. Before British left our subcontinent, they divide the Indian subcontinent into Pakistan and India base on religion. Muslim majority area would be Pakistan and Hindu majority area would be India. And sowing of seed for the rivalry between the Muslim and Hindu started. But there was a time, most of the people in the Indian subcontinent were Hindu. Children of Hindu become Muslim. In Bangladesh, almost 10% of the

He Is My Mother's Father --☺ Anwar Al-Haqq

population whose forefather came from somewhere else. My grandpa told me that his forefather came from Saudi Arabia to do business in Bangladesh and finally they settle in Bangladesh. He mentioned some of his neighbor whose forefather also from the Saudi Arabia. People started came from the Middle East or somewhere else probably before the birth of Christ. These people found the fertile land and whatever they sow, it grow and decide to settle down in Bangladesh.

Sometime I think how simple was the people in Bangladesh at the British time. People did not even feel to lock their door to sleep at night time. I heard a group of people came from the west to Bangladesh, and they did the interest business. Their business technique was like, they lend the money, and the tell the people "keep the principal amount of money and give me the interest". They did it without open any Bank. If anyone would do business like this in Bangladesh, I am sure most of them will not only loose the interest, they also would lose their principal.

My grandpa born in a village. The name of the village is Tita-hazra. Tita-Hazra is a village of the district of Noakhali. 2/3 miles west to Cho-mo-hony, the business Town for the Noakhali District's people. My Grandpa name is Mohammed Rahmat Ullah. These are the Arabic words which mean 'Mohamed is the mercy from Allah's'. With some other districts in Bangladesh, Bay of Bengal spread out from Noakhali to meet with the ocean. Noakhali is below the sea label. As Global warming will continue happen, Noakhali will go under the sea. Some time I tried to aware the people about the catastrophe the people in Bangladesh would going to face in the future. It would be under the see water one day with other country like Maldives. One day I was talking with the Jenia and Carol at the library. We were talking about Global warming.
"If global warming would continue, Bangladesh would be under the sea water".
"Really" Carol said.
"yes, it would be going to happen to us. Most of the Bangladesh is considered would go under the sea label"
Carol and Jania ware listening to me carefully.
"Can you imagine 160 million people which is more than half of the population in the USA live in a place which is size like Wisconsin, a State in the USA".

"people from Bangladesh would need to relocate to the country like in the USA, Canada, Australia even in Africa where vast area of land remain empty " I added
Carol frown her forehead and said "we are already overcrowded".
"east part of the USA is little over crowded, but west part of USA is mostly empty. It is called wild wide west. After living in a small area, if I leave the people of Bangladesh in the west, they would be wild and run before they would be tired and settle down in a corner of the western part of the USA. Eastern part of the USA also can absorb some people."
"probably in Montana" Carol said mockingly.
I understood, I would not get any support from Carol.
"you know sometime I think about the problem the people of Bangladesh would face one day and I know that no one would give the Bangladeshi to live in their country." I said
"so you already know it" carol said.
"you know 'what could solve the problem when the people of Bangladesh would live under the water'?" I asked Carol.
Carol and Jenia were listening to me carefully.
"Bangladesh and Maldives need to found a Research Institute. Like Genetic Engineering. It will create the people which would be look like a turtles. Human would have a big hard shell in their back and abdomen that sea fish like shark could not eat them. This people could live in the water and in the land."
"this could solve the people, if the genetic engineer would be success. Bangladeshi would hide their head under the hard shell" Jania said.
I looked at Jenia with amazing. I was impressed by her intelligent.
"I saw at the news that people dump the chemical at the river and there is no fish in the river of Bangladesh". Jenia said by ignoring my feeling.
"that is true. But not fully. Some of the river does not have fish any more. Because rich Industrialist in Bangladesh felt that they do not need to eat river fish".
I saw Carol want to say something. I and jenia looked at Carol.
"it would be better be a Duck. It could walk, swim and fly" Carol said.
I became bewilder again. How come duck did not come to my head!
"yea! You are right. Duck also could migrate one place to other, and it is fast. People also called them migratory bird" I said.
When Carol heard the word 'migrate', her face first become gloomy

He Is My Mother's Father -- ☺ Anwar Al-Haqq

than gave me a suspicious look. I tried to pretend that I did not notice her feeling. We remain silent for a while. I looked at Jenia to broke our silence and I continue "any way, you brought an another big problem in my attention. Genetic Engineer have to create the Enzyme inside the Bangladeshi people that they could neutralized the Industrial toxic to survive."

I took a pause and looked at Jania and started talking with emotion "I have a dream. One day my country man would be like the duck. And I have a dream. They would fly from Bangladesh and fly over the Atlantic and the Pacific. And I have a dream. They will rest at the ocean and catch fish. They would have big sharp nail at their tommy and shark keep distance from them. And I have a dream. They would reach the shore of Australia and America. And I have a dream."

I saw Carol frown her face and looking at me. And I stop my speech. "Any way come back from the genetic engineering to the reality." I said. It was 8 o'clock and we stop our conversation and I way on my way to come home. I was thinking to introduce about my country to them.

Bangladesh has six seasons. In the rainy season, whole Noakhali goes under the water. Rice field was dig up to make the pond to get a high land where homes were built. One to many homes form the 'House'. Every house has garden where Coconut tree and all the other fruit trees usually planted to grow. Green coconut water is sweet and considered the natural pure water source in the rural area of Bangladesh. Betel-nut trees grow a plenty. Peanut and other nut also produce a lot in Noakhali with the special care. Noakhali is famous for the coconut. Its people use coconut to cook all kind of curry. Noakhali people love coconut, and its people have fame for the hospitalities. Rice field was dig up to make the canal and use it soil to make the road for the people that they could walk in the rainy season. In the rainy season, water fill the rice field and the canal where the village people use boat to communicate one place the other. Most of the boat have roof to protect it passenger to save them from rain and from the fierce sun. Most of the village has the Hut where the village people exchange their product one to other. Hut is a kind of market place for the rural people. My grandpa's father had a shop in the hut and he also had an office in the Hut. The office had two rooms. One room was very private. It had two doors. One door was used to go one room to other room. And one door was used to come directly from the Hut to the private room. Other room was bigger than the private room. It also had a big door and four big benches where usually guest could sit comfortably. My grandpa's father was the Chairman of the Union Parisad. During the time of my grandpa's father, people come and request him to be the chairman for the Union Parishad. Corruption was not wide spread. A few bad people were at that time. Chairman worked for the people. People were more God fearing and simple. Bribe and stealing were considered as a serious sin. But now a day, situation is different. People run to be the chairman by spending their own money. Someone do it for the status. Someone do it to steal the people money. Government sends wheat, steal for the roof of the poor people. The chairman sales it in the market. So become a chairman is became a profitable business. So people spend a lot of money as an investment to be the chairman of the Union Parishad. The nick name of the most Chairmen is 'wheat thief'. It does not bother them. Still people say 'hello' to them respectfully. Now a day people invest heavily to be the chairman of the Union Parishad. Most of them lost their investment by loosing in the election. Then they come out and say "I just did it for the recognition. Now people know me". The candidates run for the Election to showing off their wealth and their prosperity to the people.

If we can go back to my grandfather father's time when he was a chairman, most of the Bangladesh was like a village. Only a small number of people used to live in the city. Population probably was one fourth which has right now in Bangladesh. Except a few Industrialist, those who had the paddy land, he was consider as a rich man. Most of the people had the paddy land. Ponds were full with different kind of fishes. And it was plenty. Cows, goats. Chicken and duck were raised in every house. Plenty of fruits and vegetable but there were not enough people to eat those fruits and vegetable. If one person asked for help everyone came out to help that person. Robbing house was hardly happened. That time rich man sons were the robber. They gave letter to other rich man about their demand. And most of the time their demand was met. And these robbers gave the money to the charity. And they came at day light and walked in front of the people. But now a day this real story is like a fairy tale for the most people in Bangladesh.

Everyone one want to come to the city for the living. Industrialist, politician and the organized gang member eat food in same table. People and people are every where. Over use of fertilizer, destroy the egg of the most fish and they went extinct. Competition for the resource is everywhere. Rich are getting richer and poor are getting poorer. Gang member are on control of the street and police also getting their share. Helping hands of the Bangladeshi people turned into how to give hardship one another for the limited resource has in Bangladesh. Everyone want to get it and big in portion regardless of thinking other. Moral values are deterioration. Family bonds are falling apart. One Bangladeshi is becoming the source of hardship for other Bangladeshi. Mosques are becoming full at the prayer, but the teaching of the religion does not reflect on the people's life style. Honest and weak are asked "where to escape?" But there is nowhere to escape. Most of the students are coming out from the Medical Collage, university with the certificate without having proper knowledge. And they are mostly proud of their certificate and becoming useless. Nation is approaching to lack of talented educated people.

Noakhali People Fight against Odd when no odd should be exist

One day I was walking in the street to come to home. I saw few kids about the age of 8-12. They were running and saying in Bengali "Noa-kha-lla Bo-ot, Agun Zale Pat-put". People from other distract use the word Noa-kha-lla to disrespect the people who are from the district of Noakhali. On the way I was thinking why these kids are saying this. If I translate it to English, the close meaning it would have "hey Ghost of Noa-kha-lla! There is a flame with intense fire which is making the sound of Pat-put." Some people in Bangladesh believe that there is an existence of Ghost which job is to scare the people. Bo-ot mean Ghost. Islamic scholars totally disagree with it. They say "there is no such things like Ghost to scare the people. It is the people who become the ghost". People in Bangladesh believe that ghosts also become scare when they see fire, big iron bar etc. I was asking myself "do these kids scare when they see the people who are from Noakhali. And now they want to scare the people of Noakhali by showing the fire. They want to considered the people of Noakhali as a ghost. Whatever it was, I was thinking to use it to scare the other people who were from

Noakhali. Let see if this act would have any effect to the people of Noakhali. After that it came in my mind about the sermon of the Friday prayer. The Muslim priest said what have in the Koran "Satan would enter the thought process of the people and he will order the people to slit the ears of the cows. (and without reason people will fight with each other)."

Any way come back to the story of my Grandpa's father was the chairman of the Union Parishad and his office. He used to meet with the people in the guest room. And he kept the private room very private where only the family member could go. Noakhali is connects with Dhaka, the capital, by road, train and by river. The Meghna River connects Noakhali with the rest of the country. This is one of the mighty rivers in Bangladesh. When heavy rain fall and the village and the town go under the water, this is the river which become wide open and swell up to hold all the water to drain it into the Bay of Bengal and to show it mercy. And save the people not to be drown. It is saving the people property in Dhaka and the other city which is connect with it. This river not only save the life of the Bangladeshi people not to be drown, but also the people of West Bengal, India. The water of the river Meghna when swell up, the canal and rice field and even the road of Noakhali go under the water. It is become easy to paddle the boat in the direction of the flowing of the water. But it is become some time extremely difficult to paddle the boat against the stream of the water. Boat man need help at that time. Someone needs to pull the boat against the stream of the water. It is a kind of odd situation. Any way, we the Noakhali District's people is not only the 'Fight Against the Odd' district in the nation, we are also the 'Fight Against the Odd' district's people in the whole world. Most of us do not let the obstacle to tame us. Only some of my grandpa's friends went to Dhaka and came back when they found there were hostility in Dhaka against the Noakhali people tame them. The local people of Dhaka openly said "if the trend would like this and all Noakhali people would come to Dhaka, there will be no people in Dhaka to speak in Dhaka's dialect." The people from Commilla, Mymenshing, and all the other district people also looking for the fortune in Dhaka as the Capital of the province, but Noakhali people got all the blame. Some time the Noakhali people fight against the odd where actually no odd was existed. Or they fight against the odd, when there should not have odd. I am giving an example. One day I was walking with two friends at the

He Is My Mother's Father --☺   Anwar Al-Haqq

Park near the Parliament House in Dhaka. One of my friend parents came from Mymenshing and other from Rajshahi. Mymenshing and Rajshahi are the district in Bangladesh. While we were walking at the Park, we met some of our school friends. I was a twelfth grade student at that time. When we met with our school friend, my friend from Mymenshing started talking with the Noakhali dialect. And everyone started laughing. I understood that Noakhali language entertain them. But I kept silent. Somehow these people need to entertain them. My these school friends are not from Dhaka. One of our school friend asked My Mymenshing friend "how did you learn the royal district language?" Everyone started laughing again. I understood that they came for fun. But their mouth were getting dried not to find any fun so far. Now they found something.
"Hum! Bangladeshi people calls Noakhali district is the royal district" I talked myself.
My Mymenshing friend respond "one man one day dug up 30 feet soil and I suddenly found a cave. And the first word he heard 'Honey'."
Everyone started laughing. In Noakhali, people called water as 'Honey'. In Dhaka, people call water as 'Pa-ney'. I was just listening without interrupting their fun to show my generosity and to show them that I am from a civilized district. And also the technique was to fight against the odd.
My Mymenshing friends started again "When Neil Armstrong first put his feet at the moon, he saw 5 people were sitting on there. And he went close to them. And he also hear the first word 'Honey'. Then Neil Armstrong asked them where are they from. All five responded that they were from the royal district in Bangladesh" Everyone started laughing.
"after that I decided to know the Royal District language" My Mymenshing friends added.
"a lot of time you already told this joke that Noakahli people could be found everywhere in this universe." I said.
"am I wrong?" My Mymenshing friend responded and started laughing.
Everyone started laughing with him.
"one man use the telescope to observer the sun and he found two men were sitting at the sun and were repairing something at the sun. Then he tried to listen what they were talking. And he also hears the first word 'Honey'. Tell them that this is your favorite story too" I requested my Mymenshing friend after everyone stop

laughing.

My Mymenshing friend did not say anything but smile.

"Do you know that one of my friend whose family came from the rural area of Dhaka to the City Of Dhaka and what did he say proudly?" I asked.

"yes I know it" one of them said and interrupted me.

"you know but everyone here don't know it" I added.

And I continue "that they will never let their sister to marry a boy who is from Noakhali. Even a little trace from Noakhali they would find they would make it to disqualify to be the husband of his sisters. And they think that they are one of the most respectable family in the area. And one day I found that there was not enough fun going on in their family because of the result of the final examination of their older brother. He just barely passed at the BA (Honors) examination. And I proposed to marry his sister who was two years older than me. She is the oldest and most beautiful one among his three beautiful sisters. And sound of laugh penetrated through their windows. But they kept it within their family members. But I want everyone to know it. No one knew why they were laughing except their family members. After two days of the proposal, I told all my friends " if she would marry anyone in her life that person would be 'me'. You guys already know that how happy were they to get my proposal". My message and thought were reached to their family instantly. That aggravated the situation. They laughed even more loudly. And finally they found that I proposed to marry his sister was just to bring the smile in their face; and they annoyed. To cool them down I said "I know very well that they are the one of the noble family in our area. I just check to know that do I have any qualification to propose to their family or not. And I founded that I don't. And they cool down."

Everyone looked at me, than everyone said at the same time "yes you did".

"how is your grandpa?" one of them asked me.

I looked at him with surprise. He made me to have a wrinkle in my forehead. "why he asked me suddenly about my grandpa?" I asked myself. I had a feeling to dump all my frustration forcefully on him which was accumulated last half an hour inside of me by hearing that they were making fun about Noakhlali. A lot tension developed inside of me. Joke about my grandpa's birthplace! My grandpa advised me to talk tactfully with the people. So I suppressed my feeling. And I became normal. But at the same time I had the

He Is My Mother's Father -- ☺   Anwar Al-Haqq

thought that our grandpa wants to proud for us. He does not want someone to insult us and let it to happen without being challenge. So I have to make a balance in my action.
"he is fine" I respond nicely by twisting my mouth, and almost closed the eyes and shake my head front to back.

My grandpa wants to feel proud of us. And he is always looking for it. But sometime Mr. Ansari think that my grandpa unnecessarily feel too much proud for us. What did happen after my proposal to that girl at the area where I live? In Dhaka everyone know their neighbor very well. My proposal news spread out quickly to the whole area. Mr. Ansari also was not excluded to get this news. My grandpa already got the news from Mr. Ansari. I proposed the girl to marry. Mr. Ansari raised the question about my age, qualification, and ability to support my wife. All he did to let my grandpa to feel low. My grandpa also felt 'I hamper the pride he had about his grandchildren'.

"they already told that no way they will accept the bridegroom who is from Noakhali" Mr. Ansari said to tease my grandpa.
"now they are laughing to your grandson" Mr. Ansari added.
"we will find a young and even better looking smart girl for our Rontu". my grandpa said to cover up his humiliation.
"This girl was two years in same class for 2 time. She is just beautiful. If she goes for the interview to have a job, no one will hire her. What only beauty can do? She does not known even how to talk." mockingly my grandpa said.
"when something is out of the reach they have to console them like the fox did 'grape is sour'" Mr. Ansari continually mocking my grandpa.
Mr. Ansari continued mocking to let my grandpa to feel little low and to show his pride. And my grandpa was mocking back to the girl to overcome his feeling of becoming little shame to be the grandpa of mine. My grandpa took his tongue out with the grimaces face and make sound to let Mr. Ansari that the girl has no qualification to be my wife and told to Mr. Ansari "her husband have to feed her whole life. Now a day woman also has to work to earn money. She would be like pillar of the house."
  After I heard how my grandpa mocked her and let Mr. Ansari to think about her of a useless girl, I was thinking myself "If she could know it, she would go to the roof of the building to jump down to get

rid of the feeling of a lower human being". And I also tried to understand how low my grandpa was feeling and what defensive mechanism he used to deal with it. I also was thinking how some odd things develop which does not have any explanation in the religious and moral view point such as Noakhali people considered as an outcast somehow in the city of Dhaka. One odd or sin contributed to develop many more odd or sins in the society which could destabilize the harmony in the society. As the old proverb said "to hide one crime, people sometime commit 10 crimes and it continue. Finally they would see they already committed 1000 of crimes. If people themselves admit that it was a crime and they regret that they should not do it in first place and try to correct themselves, than only people can stop to committing crime. In this situation people need high moral value to declare them that they are the one who is guilty and they need to correct themselves. If people continue committed crime, after sometime in a society there would have a chaos. Only way to prevent the chaos is to follow the religious rules and to educate the people the religious moral value and urge them to apply it every aspect of their life. Such as our prophet said that his Follower should considered as one body. One Muslim would get hurt other Muslim should feel it regardless of color, race, poor or rich, short or small, weak or strong. We need to follow the religious rule to please God. God will not judge people base on where they born. God will judge people what they do to God. Do they follow the God command or not? Every individual person is responsible for his own actions. Same way one human being should judge other human being. My grandpa taught me these time to time. Those people who put effort to make outcast the Noakhali people open the door for the Satan to play to break the harmony in the society. This action of these people would continue as long as these people and the offspring of these people will not correct themselves. Their acts would be the source for their offspring to commit thousands of sins. Or people of Noakhali when would tried to take the revenge, they will commit at least hundreds of sins. Only following strictly religious teaching could prevent it. Other district people started the heinous act such as Noakhali people should be considered as an outcast in the city of Dhaka. They did it due to lack religious teaching they put in action in their life. If they put the religious teaching in action of their life, they would put all the Muslim and non-Muslim in safe place that their words or action could not hurt other Muslims and non-Muslim. If we ask them why they think Noakhali people should be outcast in the city of Dhaka and if they answer the question honestly, people will not find any justifiable answer or people would find the jealousy or others. These people probably would tell that Noakhali people behave little differently than them. But there is no sin to be act little differently than other. Their hearts are filling with sins. I am not saying all the people of the other district are doing these heinous acts. Some of the other district people are doing it. Some people started these heinous acts probably more than 50 years ago, but we are still experience it. And probably we will experience it in the future. People may already commit millions of sin because of it. This is an example of the promise of Satan. Satan promise to make the children of Adam (PBUH) sinner. Satan found the little different one group of people to other and use it to lead the some people to commit the sin and let it to continue until today.

I was coming to home. I met with my grandpa at his store. He stood up and become very angry to see me.
"what did you tell to that girl" my grandpa asked me.
"which girl?" I asked softly.
"don't pretend to be naïve to me" grandpa said loudly to show his anger.
"you could have heart attack. Cool down"
I tried to cool him down and told him why I propose the girl. Finally he calm down and sat back to the chair and after a while he gave me a look by little twisting his neck. He looked to me with smile and his one eye was half close and other eye keep open to see me. Then he became little angry again and said "you mother already here it".
I jumped up. Fun also could bring the trouble.
"your mother would use the broom to beat you out from the house" my grandpa said.
I looked at my grandpa for help.
My grandpa called his cousin Moti and sends me to his house for two days. Before I went to Moti Grandpa's house, I took 15 small packages of chocolate from my grandpa's store. It was the best chocolate in Bangladesh. While I was taking the chocolate and put at the beg, grandpa was looking at me with discontent and disapproval. But he did not tell me anything. I did not gave much attention to his feeling.

When I knocked the door of Moti Grandpa, it was 4 o'clock in the evening. His servant opened the door for me and greeted me. I gave her one package of the chocolate. She was happy to get the chocolate package and went inside the home. I was sitting at their living room. She gave the message of my presence to the other family members of their home. After a while Moti Grandpa and his wife came to greet me. Their language were as usually like before, but I felt they were smiling little longer than they used to. Their body language made me little uncomfortable. I tried to make things normal and tactful as my grandpa taught me. I gave one pack of chocolate to Moti grandpa and one pack to his wife. I also call her 'Grandma'. Grandpa just gave me a suspicious look by holding the package of the chocolate and put the pack on the stool. Grandma became little curious.

"what is this for?" she asked me.

"I thought you could like the chocolate" I respond.

"Oh!" she said with her eyebrow up.

Then they tried to ask me about my health and the health everyone at our home. After I answer the question of the health of my grandparents, I did not give them the opportunity to ask even the health of Azim and Jamil. I told them one by one by mentioning their name to let them know that all of our family members were fine.

"everyone is fine. They are fine" I said to them with shaking my head.

I felt like it was giving them amusement to ask the health of my family members. They were using the words to talk with me but I felt they were using their secret body language to communicate with each other. And I felt little uncomfortable without making sure that indeed they were using their secret body language. I felt like Moti grandpa's wife was asking me question about my family members, but she was smiling longer then she used to and her cheek also getting little wide. I remain calm to answer their question politely the way I was taught by my parents.

After a while, grandma and grandpa went inside the home. Other family members one by one came to meet with me at the living room. I gave everyone one pack of chocolate except two of the sons of my grandpa. I respect them as my own uncle what our culture taught us. His younger son was my age. So we could share story with each other. His age made him little less respectful to me compare to his other brothers. When he came to meet with me, I also gave him a pack of chocolate. After that I looked at my beg to see how many chocolate package let in my bag. Still five more packages left to give to the family members of Moti Grandpa.

After an hour, Moti Grandpa and his wife came back again to the living room. She pretended that she did not meet with be just two hours ago.
"how are doing? How do you feel today" she asked me.
I become little bewilder. And I took a pause to try to understand the situation. And I gave her a pack of chocolate.
"oh! Chocolate" she said.
I tried to be tactful again. And I tried to behave that I just meet with her two hour ago. I felt little tension inside of me. And I tried to remove it. And I was look for words to say something to her.
"life is like chocolate" I said.
"definitely" she said with smile.
"it should be sweet like chocolate". she added after took a brief pause.

I heard before about her from my own grandma that she is little naughty. Now I tried to understand why my grandma always told Moti grandpa to bring her with him while he would come to visit our home. At dinner, I ate food with Moti grandpa and with his wife. I felt like they were trying to suppressing their funny feeling which was creating inside of them. I felt like they were trying to give me little more care then they used to. And it was unusually to cook all the good food for me. I proposed the girl for the fun, but fun was creating the tension inside of me. I did not able to interpret how people took my idea of fun as a negative or positive way. I just tried to be tactful. I bought the chocolate to ease the situation. That aggravate the situation to become worse or it had no effect at all I did not able to determine that day. But I thought surely I should not bring the chocolate.

In my absence, grandpa tried to manage everyone. My family members also do not like that family. I was lucky that my sister was not at home. She was at the college dormitory. She can't here the name of this family. While I was at Moti grandpa's house, grandpa told my grandma about this girl's story. And she told my mother. Now all family knew why I proposed that girl. My grandpa was updated everyday about the situation of that girl's family. They laugh loudly. And finally they found it was just for fun to bring the laugh in their family.

Next morning Mr. Ansari came to talk with my grandpa. He tried to bring the issue again.

"Aih-aih-aih-aih-ah, how did you grandson propose that girl?" Mr. Ansari wanted to embarrass my grandpa.

"just leave it! Just leave it!! Kids sometime do it" my grandpa said with big smile.

Mr. Ansari become first little bewildered. But said again "aih-aih-aih-aih-ah how did he do it. I do not get it?"

"just leave it! Just leave it!! Leave it!!!" my grandpa said with laughing loudly.

Mr. Ansari even more become bewildered. He did not become success to let my grandpa to feel embarrass this time. He looked at my grandpa and tried to understand the situation. He gave a suspicious look to my grandpa. After that he changed the topic. After he found my purpose of proposing the girl, he did not bring this issue again to talk with my grandpa.

I was a special guest of Moti Grandpa for two days. After two days, I came back home by get assurance from grandpa that he was able to manage my mother. With scare I entered at home. My mother did not tell me anything. My dad gave a smile to see me and asked me "how is Moti Grandpa?"

Grandpa wants to be proud for us

I know very well that I did not able to make proud my grandpa like my other sibling did. Let tell a story after I came to the USA. I came to the USA two weeks before the semester would start. I felt everyone was kind of Boss or kind of important to me. I was blindly following them. I did it because I did not know what to do. It was about the time the semester would begin. A lot of moving activity was going on throughout nearby area of the University Campus. A girl from Bangladesh came to do her Master's degree. She was in her second years. I heard her name from other Bangladeshi students I met at the campus. One day around 11 O'clock I got phone call from her. I was excited to meet a new Bangladeshi student who was senior then me. Probably she could give me good advice and could help me when I would be needed because I did not have any relative around me. She first took me to the McDonald to eat. I paid for my food and she paid for her. After ate the food, she asked me to help her to move her stuff one apartment to another. I had nothing to do.

He Is My Mother's Father -- ☺ Anwar Al-Haqq

So I instantly agreed to help her with the hope on return she would help me in the future. I just told my grandpa that I met a Bangladeshi girl and I help her to move her stuff one apartment to another. I had to use the stair to move her stuff to her new apartment. Sometime we both have to the carry the stuff together like moving her bed. One day my grandpa was listening my story with very attention. I met a girl. But he did not show me his any reaction.

Next morning my grandpa was sitting at his store. Mr. Ansari, Mr. Jalil and Mr. Matin came to the store. Mr. Ansari was trying to complain about the broken road in front of his house.

"we need to talk with the Ward Commissioner about the broken road" Mr. Ansari tried to get the attention of my grandpa.

My grandpa did not pay attention to Mr. Ansari. He was interested to tell the story about the girl I met at the USA. He was planning for last two days how to tell my story to his friends about the Bangladeshi girl I met in USA.

"Rontu called me two days ago" my grandpa said with smile.

Mr. Ansari face become little cloudy. He shows his unwillingness to listen the story.

"Rontu met a Bangladeshi girl. She is very smart and beautiful" my grandpa said proudly. Smile was in his face.

As usual, Mr. Ansari showed his unwillingness to listen the story of my grandpa's grandkids. My grandpa thinks that late marriage of Mr. Ansari and his son sometime make him uneasy to hear the stories of my grandpa's grandkids. I think probably grandpa is not right about it.

"Rontu helped her to move to the new apartment. It was better apartment then the previous one." My grandpa continued.

Mr. Ansari frowned his forehead. Mr. Jalil and Mr. Matin were just listening the story of my grandpa. In this old age they have nothing to do just to listen one other story willingly and unwilling to pass their retirement age.

"If she moved in one of my apartment, I would not ask for rent from her" my grandpa said with smile. Mr. Ansari tried to move his eyes over his forehead and gave a surprise look to my grandpa. But it did not stop my grandpa.

"Rontu was holding her bed with her in the stair. Rontu was in front and was directing her".

""Make the long story short. Our brain would pick up the missing part of the story. You do not have to tell us like" his wife is already

married"" Mr. Ansari pointed to Mr. Jalil with annoying while he was talking with my grandpa.
My grandpa gave a look to Mr. Ansari. My grandpa lost his mood to tell the story and he did not continue the story. He concentrated to read his newspaper.   There was a brief silent.
"let's go the Commissioner" Mr. Matin broke the silence.
Everyone Followed Mr. Matin.

After a weak, I talked with my grandpa. I told him about the Bangladeshi girl. She was doing Maters. My grandpa stated losing his interested to know about this girl. But he was listening to me. I told him "one day I called that Bangladesh girl five times, but she did not respond my phone call". My grandpa stayed silent.
"I talked with other Bangladeshi boys at the Campus about this Girl. They said that this girl only call the Bangladeshi boys when she need them and other time she tried to avoid them and like to spend time with other foreign people." I told my grandpa.
"I need to go to the market. I will talk with you later." My grandpa hung up the phone.

Next morning Mr. Matin, Mr. Ansari and Mr. Jalil came to the store of my grandpa.
"how is Rontu" Mr. Matin asked my grandpa.
"he is fine".
"O! that day you tried to talk about a girl which Rontu met in USA recently" Mr. Matin tried to give my grandpa the opportunity to finish his unfinished story but Mr. Ansari did not show much interest of it. And my grandpa also tried to change the topics of the conversation.
"what the Commissioner told about to repair the street" My grandpa asked Mr. Matin. Mr. Matin become little surprised.

My Grandpa's Childhood

The strong you are, you have more change to fit with the environment. There is no exception in Bangladesh. Money and the power of the people could obliterate the power of the law and the regulation. Because my grandpa was the son of the Chairman of the Union Parishad, he always got extra attention from the people. It was not difficult for him to get what he had chosen in their Union

Parishad. In the school or in college drama, main male character was for him to act regardless of the main character's age or social status. He was the all-rounder to act all the characters. A day labor to king of the old days, he was the person to act on all those characters. One day I was talking with Moti grandpa, cousin of my grandpa.
He said "From the age of 16, he was a regular movie goer."
"some time he had a thought to act in the movie". "he liked the imagination. A boy or girl. They fell in love and suddenly busted into and start singing and dancing" Moti Grandpa added.
At that time, these were the ways for the movie producer needed to show the love between boy and girl. They made a lot of plot to show the love. Some time they show in the plot 'how a girl or a boy fell in love to each other; or newlywed boy and girl what they feel after their first meeting at their bed room.'

I am just giving couple of example. A boy was working in an office and a beautiful girl came to the office to do something. Pay the bill or need any document, for example. The boy fell in love to the girl at first look. The boy had the imagination. The boy started dreaming. In the movie, it was shown that suddenly both boy and girl busted into singing and dancing. The time you need to blink your eye, the same time   was require for them to crossed all the traffic signal of the city and the crowd. And you would find the boy and the girl were in a farmer land where mustards were growing. The flowers of the mustard were swing with the breeze. So were the boy and the girl. Then the boy was running behind the girl or vice versa. Then they were in between the two Mustard firms which were divided by a road covered with the sand. The music was playing in the background which was like scratching the road to take the sand out to hover surrounding the boy and the girl. And their strike of the shoes over the sand was creating the spark when they were dancing. The song filled the whole area and making the air kind of heavy. It would give you the feeling that the entire load they were carrying in their chest, they were trying to bring that out. And air was getting heavier. After a while you were realizing that they were dancing in the valley of the mountain. They were running toward the mountain. Steepness of the mountain was not the obstacle on their way. They might sometime take the horse ride or the bike ride or just they were running. Due to the mercy of the nature, they found a plan land where they stop for a while. But the boy have to show 'he was born to carry the burden'. So he lifted the girl and started walking. After that they were dancing. But they were not feeling the thirst. And they were continuing claiming the mountain. At the tip of the mountain, they found a little plan land which was cover with the snow. That was the mercy from the nature for it two children. Snow cools down their shoes. Then it was shown in the movie that they were in an ocean where have an island and at the island there is a palace. In the balcony of the palace, they sat for a while to take a rest. The nature is getting becoming merciful to them. They started walking from the balcony. A bridge was connected from the palace to the sea beach. They were waking over the bridge. Music did not stop. But the boy took a pause and look at the girl. The girl stretched out her right hand but her elbow was just over her waist. The boy did not refuse her and hold her hand then raise her hand up his head. She gave a circle around the boy to show 'he is her center'. Then they stared walking. They came to the beach. Water of the ocean was cleaning its shore by coming as a wave. And the wave also was cleaning their feet of the couple. Then in the movie it was shown 'The boy and the girl was in the office.' The boy became very modest and kind to the girl. Eagerly doing what she was requesting. In the society, people usually say "spreading the chemical that Bond could form." Which mean boy and girl fall in love to each other after a first glance and probably they will marry each other one day.

Or the plot could be like "the girl was attacked by the villains." The hero came with a horse. His left hand was holding the rein of the horse and his right hand was raise up and was holding a sword. When he came close to the girl, the villains run away. The hero's teeth clench the horse's rein and he used his left hand to grab the girl to lift up her to the horse back and his right hand still was up his head with holding the sword and was ready to strike. After a while, the hero strike on the horse legs to stop it from running. He showed his mercy to the girl. People gave him bravo. The girl became grateful to the hero. And chemical bond started from there. "There was a lot love seen in the movie. Almost no movie was produce without showing love in Dhaka film" Moti grandpa said. Moti grandpa continued "in the ungrateful environment some people can't be very ungrateful when one also need the other. Girl saw the strength, sacrifice, and love and she does not want to miss the opportunity by neglecting the finest in quality, the hero. The society she lives where girls are looking for the protector, she found a hero who know how the raise the sword up and can strike when needed. And the hero could be the good protector. So girl also melted down."

Or the plot could be dancing. Or tell the Joke to the girl. Just try to entertain the girl. Heroes come in different time, in different form, in different shape, and in different size, and in different age, and in different personality to show the different skill to the society for the different need of our society. Those were the good example of the Dhaka's film.

I knew from Moti Grandpa that our grandpa was big fan for the Dhaka film. One day Grandpa was talking about the film and the novel with me. One point grandpa became little serious. He said "the novel bring out the people imagination and the desire. And most of the time film tried to visualize it to the people to full fill the desire. And people live with the imagination. And people love it. But some time people's desire and the imagination go beyond their purpose of their life. It took away some people from their root. Then these people just run behind their imagination and desire. They forget their purpose for their life and their root. And they become lost". Grandpa become silent and started talking again "people need to understand that they also have the limitation. When they tried to do something which is beyond their ability, they also lost." Grandpa became silent again.
After a while grandpa stated talking again "first people think they should not break the social norm and the regulation. But after sometime when some people started breaking the social norm and the regulation, people think they are on the side of wrong for a while. When someone continues stay on the side of wrong behaviors, after sometime that wrong behavior becomes the normal behavior. This way which was used to consider as an immoral act started getting recognition as a moral act such as drinking wine for example". I was listening my grandpa's advice. And still tried to understand what he tried to let me to understand. Does he mean what movie tried to show to the people for entertainment, after sometime people accept it as their way of living such a bribery, robbery etc.?

Marriage

He Is My Mother's Father -- ☺ Anwar Al-Haqq

In 1958, my grandpa married my grandma. He was 20 year old and a second year student at a local college. He was studying Bachelor of Commerce. It was two years degree program. At that time, students have to take one final examination to get the certificate. Nine months before the final examination, my grandpa saw my grandma in a school function. And he fell in love instantly according to Moti Grandpa, grandpa's cousin. "It was like a magic" Moti Grandpa said. My grandpa's father told him to hold on and let the exam to be over. But it did not convince my grandpa. He told his friends to let his father to know that marriage would not be the problem to prepare for the examination. Anyway, my grandpa's father finally arranged the marriage for his only son. It was an arrange marriage with my grandpa's choice. 1000 guests were invited at the marriage which included all his friends. Hundreds of them. Groom was bought at the bridegroom house. Next morning, a boat was rented. My Grandpa's friends collect flowers to decorate the boat. Cloth was folded around the roof to the floor of the boat to give the privacy for the newlywed couple. Curtain was given to separate the bridegroom and bride from the rest of the people. Entire grandpa's friends and some of his relative were at the bank of the canal where the boat was waiting to carry the newlywed couple for two days and let them to give time to know each other. 'Force of six men strong' was created among his friends to make sure that no one would bother them. One of them was the Moti Grandpa. He was two years younger than my grandpa. But he was the person to support my grandpa in every issue. My grandpa's decision was his decision. Anyway, that day my grandpa become unusually little serious and calm.
  "It was hard to understand his mood" Moti Grandpa said.
"he was in deep thought" Moti Grandpa added. With the best wishes of his all friends and the relatives, the boat was sailed to carry it mission, to give the good quality of private time to the newlywed couple. Sometime my grandpa came out behind the curtain and stand in the deck of the boat. Sometime he exchanges one or two words with his friends. But most of the time he was in deep thought. His friends did not bother him. Only they tried to answer, if he needed to know something. They were ready to give help. My grandpa lean on the boat roof for a while with deep thought. Then he go back behind the curtain to give the time with his newlywed bride. It was going on in the whole journey. He came out from behind the curtain and standed in the deck of the boat for a while then go back behind

the curtain. But the mood did not change. The boat started it journey in the morning and stop at the Grandpa's Grandma, mother's mother, house. They spent the night at that house. Next morning the boat started it journey. And at the evening, the boat finished it task, and came to the canal near to my grandpa's house.

Two months later. It was time to fill out the application and to pay the fees to take the final examination. My grandpa filled out the application to take the examination and paid all the fees. He was studying for the examination. Certainly it came in his mind that he would do business.
Moti grandpa said "your grandpa thought that certificate only need to apply for the job. But knowledge is needed to do the business which he have already. He knew in and out of the books. So he decided to not to take the examination."
"My uncle like fell from the sky to hear this" Moti Grandpa added. My grandma's father did not support the idea as Moti grandpa told me. Anyway, my grandpa stayed in his decision and went to Dhaka to do the business and left behind his wife, parents and four sisters. Some of his friends made comment "after month or two when the local people of Dhaka would put him in a boat in the river of Buriganga and would say "out," and the stream of the water would float to bring him in the river Meghna, we would pick him up from there". Noakhali is situated on the bank of the Megna river.

New Born to Childhood

Sometime Moti grandpa told us the story how our grandpa put his father in trouble. Because he was the only son of his father, less punishment's decision he faced in his life from his father. My grandpa's first three siblings were girl. Grandpa's father was expecting to have a son. Son would carry the family tradition and usually takes care the parents. It was the condition of the society at that time. When my grandpa's father looked at his own wife and his mother, he knew very well the fate of a woman at that time. They were treated like the water. People threw out the water and it was gone. Same way the girl was. Father gave them marriage. They went to their husband house. And their husband house became their permanent address. Sons have to carry the family fame and name. After became father of three daughters, my grandpa's father became father of a son. That made him very happy. And he invited

the whole village and slaughtered two cows to cook good food for them. They pray for the happy and prosperous life for my grandpa. My grandpa's father was the chairman of the Union. Some of them wish my grandpa would be the leader of the country. But people's wish did not made any appeal to my grandpa. He did not grow up as a disciplined boy. Whatever came in his mind that drive him. When he was a 10 years old boy, he was playing with two of his friends in a field where Tall Species of Grass grow. It was winter season and consider as the dry season in Bangladesh. Usually there is no rain in the winter season in Bangladesh. Tall species of Grass is the of green leaf which is 3 to 4 inch wide and become up to 2 to 4 feet tall. Rural people (in Bangladesh we divide the rural area in small section which we called village. Some village form an Union.) uses it to make the roof of the house. This leaf even looked green, but in sunny day it could easily flame up to burn. While my grandpa was playing on that field where the Tall species of grasses were growing, he saw a porcupine was sunbathing. Porcupine became disturbed by seeing my grandpa and his friends. But it quickly went to it burrow. It did not save the porcupine not to be disturbed any further. All three of them tried to bring out the porcupine from the burrow. They used the bamboo stick to pock the porcupine to bring out from the burrow. But they failed. Finally it came to the head of my grandpa and he proposed "let bring the straw and put it on the burrow then light it up". Everyone agree with my grandpa. They brought the straw and put in the burrow and light it up. Quickly the Tall species of Grass caught the fire and the fire spread out the whole field. The village people came and finally able to bring the fire under control after whole Tall grass field was burned. This field was owned by the father of my grandpa. My grandpa turned his green grass field into the fume. Grandpa's father was at the market and in his office. News went to his office. He reacted that it was a great loss for him. He was planning to sale the grass for money and the money he saved last one year, he would use those money to buy a small plot of land. He already talked with the land owner about it. "who put on fire at my field" he asked the messenger angrily.
"your son" the messenger said softly.
Grandpa's father instantly took the decision how he would punish his son and said angrily "I would catch him and slam him over the ground."
Grandpa's father need to take him over his head and slam him at the ground forcefully if he wanted to do what did he said which I know

from my observation.

My grandpa's father put his hand over his forehand and remains silent for a while. Then he said again "I would beat .." He did not complete the sentence. The messenger came home and told the grandpa's mother. Grandpa's grandma heard it. She was old and fragile. She used stick to walk one place to other and most of the time she lie down at her room. My grandpa's mother already went to Moti grandpa's home even the whole family went for vacationing in Moti Grandpa's maternal grandpa's house. She knew that her husband would be very mad. My grandpa's grandma came out from her room to save her grandson. My grandpa was hiding in his grandma's room. My grandpa's grandma was not concern about the loss of the property. She was concern about her grandsons. She said "my grandchildren would put me at the grave after I would die and my grandchildren would pray for my soul not to be punished by God." She was walking at the courtyard for a while then she was sitting on over a chair. It was going on until her son came home. She was doing it that her son could see her first before he could meet anyone else. It was the norm in the society at that times that son and daughter not to raise the voice over their old parents. My grandpa's father entered house and he was looked angry. But when he saw his mother, He cooled down. He became little shock to see his mother. Usually someone was with her always. But she was sitting herself at the courtyard. My grandpa's father looked around. He saw his daughters were observing the situation from far and little sacred.

"where is everyone. You are sitting here yourself" my grandpa's father asked his mother. He rushed to come close to his mother. He knew very well that why his mother was sitting at the courtyard. She first asked "how was his day and his business". Like a good son he was responding "good". His mother told "kids sometime do mistake. If they do not do mistake how would they learn". My grandpa's father was just listening what his mother was telling him. "don't stay mad to Rahmat" my grandpa's grandma told his son. My grandpa's father just shake his head. He just said because of his mother, he did not able to discipline his son. If my grandpa's father could discipline his son according to his desire, we may experience the different outcome. We would find our grandpa in finest in quality. And I have to write his story differently than I am writing right now.

To fulfill the wishes of their grandma, every Ramadan Grandpa, Moti Grandpa and his brother went to village and slaughter a cow and cook good food for their neighbor and for the needy people. Muslim priest came to lead a prayer for the peace of the soul of their dead relatives and the Muslims who died from the day of Adam (Peace be upon him) until today.

Settled in Dhaka

After giving the hard time to his father, my grandpa left him in the village and came to Dhaka to start a new life. My grandpa stared small construction business in Dhaka. He took subcontract from the contractors who were enlisted contractor of the government. He rented one room. After six months, he went to Noakhali and bought my grandma to Dhaka. My grandma liked the boat journey. So my grandpa took steamer to come to Dhaka. After the steamer reached to Sadarghat at Buriganga River, Dhaka, they took off from the steamer. Two luggage were with them. On the way to their room from Sadarghat, my grandpa tried to hold my grandma's hand to walk. My grandma became shy. She have Borka which is use as a Hijab in Bangladesh.

"No one know us here" my grandpa tried to assure my grandma. But my grandma did not feel comfortable to walk hand on hand with her husband. They took a scooter to come to their room. This was the beginning of their journey to establish their root at Dhaka. And they founded their permanent root.

Retire Life

More than 48 years doing the construction business, grandpa quit his construction business and now he runs a small Grocery Store. The store is in the first floor of his building. There also have a place where six/seven people can sit down. He usually goes to the store sometime to read the newspaper and to meet with his friends. The store is run by his distant nephew. My grandpa used to be a Government Contractor before he retired. Two years ago he had a contact to build a building in the Mountain area of the Chittagong, second biggest city in Bangladesh. One day he had a severe diarrhea at the mountain. Now his children do not want him to do

He Is My Mother's Father -- ☺   Anwar Al-Haqq

the business. Diarrhea cut his construction career cut short. His children think it is time for him to retire. He already did enough for them. Educated them and own four buildings in Dhaka and each bulding has more than 16 apartments. He rented all those apartments. Now his full time job is to enjoy the family life as long as he would be in this world with good health. And he also does not want to miss any opportunity to enjoy the family life. But I saw there is a change in his life. He is becoming more religious.

When I was in Bangladesh, I saw him when he was with his grandsons his temper shoots up in a second. And also come down quickly. But he was not a person that age could tame him like the most other old people. He is not a person who could become fretful. His behaviors was little different with his granddaughters.
I am giving an example. One year and eight months ago my grandparents was sitting at the living room. After a while Jolly came to the living room and sat next to grandpa. He was reading newspaper. Grandpa was sitting in a sofa and was sewing a cloth. Jolly read the newspaper for a while then she said to grandpa is whispering voice "let's bother her". Jolly indicated to grandma. Grandpa smile himself behind the newspaper and pretend that he did not hear anything what Jolly said to him.

After I got the US Student Visa, his behaviors change. There was time when whatever I did was intolerable to him. But after I got the Visa, I become more tolerable to him.

Twenty second December: in the morning, I was sitting in the living room with my grandparents. I came to Bangladesh after one and half years and I want to spend time with my family members. Grandpa was reading the News Paper. He sat comfortably by leaning in his chair. My cousins, the youngest son of my uncle and his name is Azim, came to the room. Azim sat right to the Grandma and pick up one newspaper then he leaned on the chair to feel comfortable. Grandpa gave a quick look at him by lowering his newspaper over his eye glasses with little disapproval. Azim was reading the Newspaper without giving much attention to grandpa. After that my other cousin, son of my aunt and his name is Jamil, came to the room. My grandpa also lower his newspaper and give a quick look to him. He sat left to my grandma.
Azim separated a few pages of newspaper and offered to Jamil. My

He Is My Mother's Father -- ☺ Anwar Al-Haqq

grandpa's distance nephew entered the living room and said "I need to go to the market. I have TK. 10000 short this week (US $150)." "last week also have TK 9000 short" my grandpa said with surprise and shake his head.
This is not the good news for my grandpa at all. Every week there have a shortage of money at the store. He has to added money to run the shop. He collect rent from the apartment. One portion of money he collected as a rent he needs to give as a subsidy to run the store.

"I told grandma that if he does not want to run the construction business, at least he can concentrate to run the grocery business" Azim said.
My grandpa down the Newspaper and looked at him with annoying. Grandma looked at Azim with smile but was not shown to agree with him. I found that whatever grandma or someone else such as my brother said before that Azim and Jamil repeated to grandpa.
My grandma said "did your grandpa tell you not to give him advice? Hardhead. Don't want to listen to anyone."
Grandpa became discomfort and looked at my grandma. My grandpa's nephew left the living room. Grandpas shake his head. Then grandpa stood up and left the newspaper on the table and said "lets go and see any big fish has in the market. New seasonal vegetable started coming in the market".
 Grandpa left the room with little worrying.
 "Every week I have to add money from his pocket to run my shop" Grandpa talked himself.

2 O'clock at the evening Grandma, Jamil and Azim were at the roof of the building. Grandma was folding the quilt which was on the sun for whole day.
"Your grandpa would have good night sleep when he sleep at the warm quilt" Grandma said.
Azim and Jamil were listening and grandma was talking. "take these pillows" grandma pointed to the Jamil.
Jamil picked those pillows and put those pillows on top of his head. Grandma let Azim to carry the quilt. They were very eager to follow their grandma. Jamil and Azim were carrying the pillows and the quilt respectably, and grandma was walking behind them from the roof of the building to the stair.

He Is My Mother's Father -- ☺ Anwar Al-Haqq

Grandpa was coming back from the mosque after the Asar prayer. Instead of offer his prayer to his lord at his home grandpa of offer his prayer at mosque with a congregation to multiply the reward to 27 times. Still he had the cap in his head. He entered the Gate of the building and walked to the building balcony. Grandma was sitting with Tiza, daughter of my elder brother. She just waked up from the nap. Still felt sleepy. Her face was on the lap of my grandma who was sitting on a small table. My grandpa sat on a chair.
"where is her grandma?" Grandpa asked by pointing to the Tiza and took the newspaper to read.
"Her grandma went to the collage to attend to the meeting" grandma reply. Jolly, daughter of my uncle, and Lilly, daughter of my aunt, entered the balcony.
"grandpa" Lilly said loudly. When Lilly saw Tiza, she went to Tiza. Grandpas took his eyes off from the newspaper and look at her with smile and started reading the newspaper again. Jolly sat next to the grandpa.   Lilly tried to play with Tiza. Tiza annoyed.
"after waked up from nap, she usually does not have a good mood. It's take time for her good mood to come back" Grandma said to Lilly.
Grandpa's eyes were in the newspaper and asked Jolly softly "do your think that your grandma should not participated to their 'Root Meeting' this year?"
Jolly said "she can participate to their so called 'Annual Root Meeting'".
Grandma looked at the Jolly with smile.
  Jolly said with little sarcastically "all her love for her root."
"Even Rontu came to visit us from USA" Grandpa said.
"I think she could go. It is only for 4 days" Jolly responded.
Grandpa shacked his head. Grandma raised her head with smile. She got Jolly's support. She took out Chocolate from the edge of her Sari and gave one to Jolly then one to Lilly.
"if they eat Chocolate, they would lose their teeth". Grandpa said.
Jolly looked at Lilly and said "half of the grandpa's store chocolate goes to your tummy. Show Grandpa that chocolate does not have any harmful effect to the teeth".
Lilly went in front of Grandpa and open her mouth widely with the sound 'haaa'. Grandpa lowered his head and gave a quick look to her teeth then looked at her with smiling and said "do you think I am sitting here to see your worm eaten teeth? Go away from my face."
Jolly stood up and put her hand to the shoulder of Lilly "Don't

worry. It is grandpa's trick to discourage you not to eat his store chocolate. You already shown him that chocolate have no harmful effect to your teeth. What a teeth! If you just see the food, you eat everything. Gappuush! Gupoosh! but your teeth did not scare grandpa. If you teeth don't scare grandpa, nothing will scare him. Let's go to the roof of the building." Jolly told Lilly and both left the balcony.

"did Lilly eat that many chocolate?" grandpa asked with surprise.

"eat two/three chocolates. Not half of your store's chocolate." grandma respond.

Grandpa's cell phone rung. Grandpa took his cell phone from his Panjabi pocket.

"Hello" grandpa said.

"Oh! Mr. Ansari. I will be down their within a minute."

Grandpa stood up and was about to walked to the down stair to meet with his two friends.

Grandma said "Mina will bring tea and cookie for you soon". Mina was hired to help to do the household job.

"I will drink tea at the restaurant" Grandpa said and left the balcony.

At the downstairs, grandpa met with his friend. All of them are retire person. Grandpa, Mr. Ansari and Mr. Matin were walking in the street. Grandpa stood up in front of a Constructing site of a building. It looked like they just start to build a building. Three labors were working on the site. One labor shake the cement beg to get out of all the cement from the beg. Cements were hovering surrounding them. Grandpa move close to the labors and stood up again at the construction site.

"how many floor are you going to build in this place" grandpa asked a labor.

"five floors." A worker responded after he stood up from the bending position of the mixing of the cement.

"2200 square ft space roughly" grandpa talked himself.

"What is the ratio of the cement and the sand are you mixing?" grandpa ask.

"seven bucket of sand with one bucket of cement" other worker responded.

All the labors showed that they were more interest to talk with grandpa then to do their work. Grandpa, Mr. Ansari and Mr. Martin started walking. Grandpa was giving the estimate how many begs of

cements and how many tons of iron rod would be need to   complete the building.
"price of the rod and cement increase at least 5% compare to last two years" Mr. Ansari said.
Grandpa shake his head and said "yes! you are right. Cost will be 5% higher than my estimate to complete the building".
"Did you see that I just asked the labors how many floor they would build and all the labors were eager to answer the question? If they would work like this, my estimate even have to increase 5% more. You needed to stay with them to get the service out from them." grandpa said.
"if I will go to the Motijel, a commercial zone in Dhaka, with Matin and take the bus, probably I will hear 'Farmgate! Farmgate!!'" Mr. Ansari said and pushed Mr. Matin gently. Farmgate is a place in a Dhaka.
Mr. Matin respond with laugh "I just worked six months to collect bus fare when I came first from Noakhali to Dhaka and that time Fox were running in the Farmgate. Anyway, at that time there also had a bus conductor to help the driver to collect the bus fair, but it was not necessary to call the people and let them to know that where the bus would go.".
Grandpa looked at them but did not say anything. The sun is almost going to be set. They started walking to the mosque   for the Magrib prayer.

Went to watch Drama

Grandpa, Mr. Matin and Mr. Ansari came out from the mosque. They started walking. On their way, Grandpa saw Azim and Jamil were on the street. They were talking and walking on the street. Grandpa's face became little gloomy and serious to see them. He stood up. So were Mr. Ansari and Mr. Matin.
"they supposed to be at home. What are they doing here?" grandpa talk himself.
Mr. Ansari told "their final examination is over. No need to study."
Grandpa did not pay attention to Mr. Ansari. Then he stared walking toward Azim and Jamil.
"Grandpa" Jamil and Azim said loudly.
"both of you supposed to be at home" grandpa said.
"we went to play Cricket. We are on our way to home." Azim said.
Grandpa little cooled down. But he was serious. Grandpa walked to

the restaurant. Everyone followed him. They sat in a table for six people. Grandpa, Mr. Ansari, and Mr. Matin sat one bench and Grandpa was in middle. Azim and Jamil sat the other bench. Grandpa still looked very serious. Azim and Jamil did not pay much attention to it. They were in little good mood to came with the Grandpa to eat tea at the restaurant. Mr. Ansari ordered for tea and Samosa for everyone. Grandpa looked at Azim and Jamil with annoy. Again they did not pay him that much attention about his seriousness.
"grandpa! Called your daughter and let her know that we are with you. Otherwise she will not let us to sleep at home tonight". Jamil said.
Grandpa pretended that he did not hear anything.
"grandpa" Azim said loudly with surprise.
Grandpa unwillingly took out his Cell phone from his Panjabi's pocket. He shown that this was the last think in the earth he can do which is to keep the request of Azim and Jamil. Then he gave a hard look to them. He does not want to do it. But He was doing it. No interest to call his daughter for Azim and Jamil. Azim and Jamil become little happy to get grandpa's support.

Grandpa was looking to Aziz and Jamil with annoying while he was pressed the number to call his younger daughter. Suddenly his face changed. Smile and affection was expressing in his face. His tone went down.
"this is you dad. Jamil and Azim are with me. And they will come home with me."
"ok"
Grandpa hanged up the cell phone. He put his cell phone in his pocket. While he put the cell phone in his pocket, he gave them a serious looked and his face went back to the previous condition. It was like while he was talking with his younger daughter, all his sympathy to the people were tickling down to his cell phone and after he finished his talking with his daughter, he sympathy for the Azim and Jamil dried out.
"thank you grandpa" Jamil said with smile.
Grandpa just shake the head with little madness. He gave them impression that they obliged him to do it. He showed that he was not happy about it.
"what did the aunt said? Will she tell my Mom?" Azim asked.
"I hope I will be not to force to request my daughter again. Keep this in your mind." grandpa responded.

He Is My Mother's Father -- ☺   Anwar Al-Haqq

Tea and Samosa came. They were eating the Samosa. While eating, they continue their conversation.
"a drama will be played tomorrow at our school. You all are invited to attend the drama" Azim said.
Grandpa become little easy. But did not become completely normal. Become little thoughtful.
"off-course we will go to watch the drama tomorrow. We already got the invitation card. Mr. Jalil also will be with us" Mr. Matin respond.
After finished the tea and the samosa, Grandpa walked to the cash counter to pay the bill. They are the regular customer for this restaurant. Mr. Ansari tried to pay the bill. But Grandpa paid the bill and walked to home. Jamil and Azim followed him.

Next morning, grandpa picked his Salayani, a special kind of Coat man use in Bangladesh, Pajama and Panjabi from the Laundry. After that he walked to come to home. At home, he walked to the living room. He put his Salayani, Pajama, and Panjabi on there. He comfortably sat on his chair. In Bangladesh, people called it 'Easy chair'. People could sit comfortable. It is kind of half bed and half chair. It has handle for to support the arms and hands. There is only one 'Easy Chair' in the living room. This is special chair only for the grandpa. No one usually sit on that chair. Grandpa was reading the newspaper. He was in happy mood than usual. But he was not saying anything. No one also asking him any question. He looked proud. Satisfaction was in his face. Azim was coming toward the living room. Grandpa became little serious. He showed that he was in full concentration to read the newspaper.
"Grandpa" Azim asked.
Grandpa raised his head and shown that Azim disturbed him in reading the newspaper. He did not respond to Azim and put concentration to read the newspaper. Azim stood for a while with surprise.
"hoou! what did I do?" Azim asked himself.
"ooohhhh!" Azim pretend that he found the answer why Grandpa was bothered.
"grandpa! Which movie is now playing at the Ananda Theater?" Azim asked.
Grandpa felt even more disturbed.
"opph! He did not memorize the whole newspaper yet." Azim said

and left the room.

In the evening, Grandpa, Mr. Jalil, Mr. Ansari, Mr. Matin were walking to the school to watch the drama where Azim and Jamil study. There was a mosque at the school. Drama would start after the magrib prayer. After offer their magrib prayer, they entered with other people into the school theater. Screen was down. After a while the screen was pull up. All the actors and actors were introduce by a teacher of the school. Azim had to play as the main actor and Jamil had to play the main supporting actor. Mr. Jalil Grandson was the villain in the drama. Then the screen was pull down. After a while, screen was pull up. Drama started.
A girl was walking to the school in a street. She has a back pack. Mr. Jalal's grandson was with two of his friends and ask her "are you alone?"
"my mother told me not to talk with stranger in the street" girl respond and started walking.
Mr. Jalal grandson walked to grab her hand and said in rude voice " you insult me. Do you know the consequence of it? Ha-ha-ha-ha. My name is Muku. No one in this town show the courage to stand in front of me. I do not kill the chicken and I do not eat the chicken. Ha-ha-ha-ha-haaa." Muku laughed loudly.
girl became scared.
Jamil and Azim were walking on that way. Jamil stood up.
 "it looked to me this girl is our neighbor" Jamil told Azim.
They run to the girl.
"take the handoff from the girl" Azim said with shouting voice.
Jalil grandson looked at one of his companion and said "Tuku, can you teach him how many paddy need to get how many rice"
Tuku went toward Azim with fighting mood. Fight started. First Azim and Jamil got few punched and got bruises. Then they bit the Mr. Jalil's grandson and his gang. They run away.
"thank you" girl said.
"we just did our moral duty" Azim respond.
"if you were not here, I don't know what could happen to me" Girl said and started crying.
Azim went to give her the consolation and put his hand to the girl head and told "if they bother you just let me know. I will bit them out from this city."
Girl took the napkin from her back pack and clean Azim's wound. Azim become little absent minded. He did good job.

"your class will started soon" Jamil said to girl.
Girl walked to the school. And the girl looked back couple of times to Azim and Jamil. Azim and Jamil also looked at her. Girl, Jamil and Azim look at each other. Girl tried to say how grateful she was to them. Azim and Jamil showed how proud they were to save a girl from the street boys who have nothing to do but to bother the girl unnecessarily.
"thank friend" Azim said.
"No problem. For friend I would sacrifice my life" Jamil said.
"This also my duty to help you to do the good deed for the society" Jamil added.
Grandpa was enjoying the drama and watching it with deep concentration. He was amaze, but suppressed his feeling. The drama was about how the school girls are bothered by the street boy and what the society should do about it.

The drama ended. Grandpa, Mr. Jalil, Mr. Ansari, and Mr. Matin were walking to come home. Grandpa became proud for his grandsons.
""let them to come to home tonight. I need to beat them. Friend! Moral duty!. Only need to beat them. Become hero." Grandpa was talking while walking. Mr. Jalil felt little low but was not talking. Mr. Ansari and Mr. Matin were looking out of curiosity to grandpa.

Next Morning grandpa was reading the newspaper at his shop. A customer came. He bought two bottles of Pepsi, cookie.
Customer asked "how much?"
"65 Taka" shopkeeper respond.
"why 65 taka?"
"20 Taka for two Pepsi"
"I know that" customer said.
"20 Taka for the deposit of the Pepsi bottle, when you will return the bottle, I will give you back 20 Taka. For the customer who drinks Pepsi at the store, we do not ask for the deposit of the Pepsi bottle".
"oh" customer said. And he gave 65 Taka and left. Grandpa was listening their conversation while reading the newspaper. Mr. Matin, Mr. Jalil and Mr. Ansari came to the store. They greeted each other.
"how was the drama last night?" grandpa asked
"good! Very good drama. Azim and Jamil were excellent." Mr. Ansari responded.

He Is My Mother's Father -- ☺   Anwar Al-Haqq

Mr. Jalil felt little embarrassed.
"Moral duty. Only need to beat them. They are friend. Want to sacrifice." grandpa said.
Mr. Matin whispered to grandpa "Mr. Jalil felt little embarrassed. Talk something different."
"Oh" grandpa said.
"I told my grandson to concentrat to his study. But he is not listening to me. He looked like a hero. If he studies hard, he would be selected to be the hero." Mr. Jalil said.
"he looked like a villain, and was selected to be the villain" Mr. Ansari respond.
Mr. Jalil even became more embarrassed.
"what are you doing at the park? I asked my grandson. You supposed to be at school right now" Mr. Jalil said.
My grandpa tried to change the topic.
"I heard you have some time stomach pain. I will tell my grandson Montu about you. He is the best doctors among his friend. I will be not surprise to hear that he would be selected as the best doctor in the nation. Don't worry about his fee. Just tell him that I send you to him."

Mr. Jalil pretended that he had little stomach pain right now.
"sometime I have pain in my right side. I go to the local pharmacy to see the doctor. He gives me the tablet. Sometime pain go away. Sometime don't. Doctor is a quack" Mr. Jalil said.
"don't worry. My grandson Montu was in top in his class. If a patients just walks in front of him he can tell what the problem is. He don't give that many tablet like other doctors. They don't know what the problem is. Give five/six tables. If one could work. Rest they left for the god mercy" grandpa said.
Mr. Ansari was looking at my grandpa out of curiosity to see how proud my grandpa was about his grandson and smiling without saying any things.
"yes. I heard some doctor have special power in their hand. They just touch the patients and all the diseases run away from the patients." Mr. Ansari said.
My grandpa gave him a look to show him that he did not like his comment.
"My daughter would come to visit me. Let see if there have any good and big fish in the market" Mr. Matin told and stand up to leave my grandpa shop.

Mr. Ansari and Mr. Jalil followed him.
"don't forget to see my grandson at his office" my grandpa told to Mr. Jalil.
"I will not" Mr. Jalil said while he was leaving my grandpa's store.

Mr. Jalil at my Brother's Medical Office

At the evening, Mr. Jalil went to my brother Montu office to see him. He was waiting with 7/8 patients. Three doctors share an office. Next to their office there is a pharmacy. My brother assistant called Mr. Jalil and took him to the examination room. The assistant was very nice to Mr. Jalil. Mr. Jalil was waiting for my brother. Mr. Jalil was the friend of my grandpa. In Bangladesh, usually the doctors do not show that much professionalism. If that person is known to them, sometime they would not maintain their professionalism. If that person is the friend of the grandpa, it is out of question to show him professionalism. We called our grandpa's friend also grandpa. Calling by name is kind of disrespect to an older person in Bangladesh. Even a person is not a relative, but he is an older person, we called them 'Bhai' as Brother, 'Apa' as a sister, uncle, aunty, grandpa, grandma.

My brother knocked the room and ask for permission to come inside the room. Mr. Jalil gave my brother permission to come inside the room. My brother came inside the room.
"grandpa! How are you?" my brother asked.
"good!" Mr. Jalil responded and was about to saying something.
"my grandpa called me to let me know that you are coming. He called me two times about you. My grandpa thing something is very serious going on inside of your body and needs immediate intervention. And he told me to give you a special care" my brother was talking with cordially and with smile.
Mr. Jalil felt little special.
"he also called me and let me to know that only you would understand what my problem is. Other doctor will not understand my disease. They will only know how to prescribe six/seven different kind of tablet and ask for God's mercy" Mr. Jalil said.
"what can I do for you?" my brother asked.
"I have stomach pain some time. My older brother died in colon cancer." Mr Jalil respond.
"how long do you have these problem?"

"one years".
"anything did you do that make you feel better?"
"sometime I take aspirin. It does sometime work. Sometime it doesn't. When my brother had colon cancer one and half years ago, he took the aspirin for pain. Do you think I have cancer?" Mr. Jalil looked worried when he respond to my brother questions.
My brother gave him a look and let him to understand that he was taking the matter seriously to know what his problem was.
"I do not know yet. I will examine you and do some test to make sure that you do not have colon cancer"
"did you ever have a colonoscopy?" my brother asked.
"what is colonoscopy?"
"it is an instrument to looked inside of you intestine. Did you ever do that?"
"no. never"
"you are 68 years old, I think you should do the colonoscopy."
Mr. Jalil got little assure. My brother thoroughly examined him.
"I felt sometime a lump in here" Mr. Jalil shown my brother his left side of the abdomen while my brother was doing the physical examination. My brother tried to feel the lump.
"No! I did not feel any. Let see other doctor can find the lump. Just wait for a minute." My brother responded and went out the examination room.
On the way he met Dr. Mia.
"I have a patient for you to do the physical examination" my brother told Dr. Mia.
"he may have somatoform disorder" my brother whisper to Dr. Mia. Dr. Mia became enthusiastic to see Mr. Jalil.
"his son is a politician and making a lot of money from his business. A happy man." My brother whispered to Dr. Mia.
Then they both enter the room. Dr. Mia suppressed his feeling. My brother introduced Dr. Mia to Mr. Jalil. Dr. Mia took the permission to examine Mr. Jalil.
"where is the lump you feel in your abdomen? Dr. Mia asked.
"Just here" Mr. Jalil showed his left side of the abdomen. Dr. Mia tried to feel the lump.
"I did not feel any lump in your abdomen. We need to follow you up. I will be in touch with Dr. Montu to know your health. Bye now" Dr. Mia told Mr. Jalil and left the room.
"Physical examination is normal so far." my brother said. Mr. Jalil become little assured.

"I am going to make an order to do endoscope and colonoscopy for you. Is that be O.K for you?"
"that will be O.K."
Mr. Jalil wait for a while. After that asked "are you going me give me any medication?"
"Oh, medication" my brother said. He took his prescription pad. And he wrote down only to eat 2-3 Vitamin C tablet a day. Mr. Jalil did not understand. You do not need prescription to buy these tablets. Continue this tablet. After I will get all the result of your test, I will discuss with you if you need anything else or not. So we done for today. Let see I can get Vitamin C tablet for you from the pharmacy. They walked to the pharmacy. My brother told the Pharmacy assistant to give 20 vitamin C tablets. Mr. Jalil is the friend of my grandpa. So he is also a special patient for my brother. Mr. Jalil wanted to pay for the Vitamin C. But my brother did not let him to pay. "bye for today. Don't forget to do the colonoscopy and endoscope" my brother said.
"I will not" Mr Jalil said and left the pharmacy. My brother went back to see the other patient.

Next morning my grandpa was reading the newspaper in his store. Mr. Jalil came to the store and gave a look inside the store to see that my grandpa was at the store or not. He saw my grandpa was sitting inside the store and walked to come close to him. He sat in a bench next to grandpa. Mr. Jalil was talking and grandpa was listening to him. Grandpa's eyes were in the newspaper. Mr. Jalil seemed to be worried.
"I am on my way to the hospital. You are right. Your grandson told me yesterday that I may have serious health problem. Doctors need to put the instrument in my abdomen to know what it is. I told my son about my health" Mr. Jalil said.
My grandpa became proud because what he said that was the case.
"what did you tell your son?" my grandpa ask softly with smile while he was reading the newspaper.
"I told my son that what Mr. Rahmat said that is it. I may have serious health problem".
Mr. grandpa even became more prouder.
"then what did your son said?" my grandpa asked while he was pretending that he was reading the newspaper.
"dad don't worry for money. See the doctor and follow them. I am going to do colonoscopy today" Mr. Jalil responded.

"good! Good! We know that you have a good son. We are proud of him.
I talked about you with Mr. Ansari and Mr. Matin. They were impressed to know that what I was suspecting that is it. They are worried about you. They said that if a disease could be found in earlier stage that disease some time could be curable. They are proud that I was able to give you an earlier warning." My grandpa said.
My grandpa took a pause. Mr. Jalil looked worried.
"When do you have appointment to do the colonoscopy?" my grandpa asked sofltly.
"10 O'clock this morning" Mr. Jalil said and looked at his watch.
"it may be colon cancer" Mr. Jalil added and looked worried.
He stood up and remains standing for a while. He looked worried.
"I have to go" Mr. Jalil said and was about to leave the store.
My grandpa stood up and put the newspaper on the table, and put his right hand on his shoulder to give him the consolation "let me know the result of the test. Don't worry too much. If time comes we have to go back to our lord. We should not be regrets what our lord decide for us."
"I will let you know test result" Mr. Jalil said.
"I talked with my grandson last night. He also told me the same. You need to do the colonoscopy "grandpa said and inhale a big breath.
"I have to run." Mr. Jalil said and left the store.
While he was leaving the store, he looked worried that he was fighting for his life.

A Proud Grandpa

"people usually said that a dog of an educated family also are educated" my grandpa talk himself.
  My grandpa took the newspaper from the table and left the store. He kept the Newspaper under his arm. On the way to his house, Grandpa met Mr. Asif, a tenet. My grandpa's face became little gloomy. Mr. Asif gave a big smile to see my grandpa. That did not able to change the mood of my grandpa.
"you did not pay the rent for last two months" grandpa asked with seriously.
"my son send the money order from UAE last week. When it will be cash, I will pay your rent." Mr. Asif said softly and gently.
"when you rented the apartment, you made a written agreement that

you will pay the rent within the first week of the month."
"I am aware of the agreement." Mr. Asif told and showed his guilty feeling about not to able pay the rent according to the agreement. Without saying anything, my grandpa walked to the apartment. Mr. Asif looked at him. Mr. Asif tried to understand the seriousness of the situation.

Grandpa went to the living room. And he sat in his easy chair. He tried to cool down. He was looking at his newspaper. My elder brother entered the living room. He sat down next to grandpa without saying any think. He picked a newspaper. A lot of time they could just sit down without exchange a word. Grandpa was talking while he was reading the newspaper.
"Mr. Jalil said what I was suspecting that happened to him. He has a serious health problem" my grandpa said slowly.
"I feel sorry for him" my grandpa added.
My brother first tried to say something then he controlled himself. He thought for a while.
"yea! It looks serious. But I did not tell you last night that how serious it is. We are trying to find it out" my brother said.
Grandpa took a pause. They did not talk for a while. His mood changed.
"Rontu" grandpa said slowly.
"yes! Grandpa" my brother responded.
"Mr. Asif is not giving my rent for last two months. It also happened before. He thinks if he just give me a big smile, he could able to manage me."
"smiling alone can't manage our grandpa, he should know it very well" my brother said.
"if he do again, I will tell 'who care your smiling.' Give me the rent" grandpa said.
"that's right. Money use to pay the rent, not the smile"
"do you think it is time to hire someone to take his stuff out from my apartment. I think it is time to give him a lesion "how many paddy need to get how many rice". I will call my nephew to bring his police force to take him out from my apartment." grandpa said.
My brother become little startle when he was listening grandpa.
"it happened to him before and his son sent the money and he paid you the rent. Let see this time. He is very nice person. He don't talk with people without smiling" my brother said.
"do you think so? He becomes nice and gives me smile. These are

the technique he uses not to pay me the rent. One time I told him that my nephew and my brother-in-law are the police office. It did not work. I think I need to go for action. When straight fingers can't bring the butter, we need to make a curve on the fingers to bring out the butter from the pot" grandpa said.
"sometime people could have problem. We need to understand their problem" my brother said.
"Mr. Asif needs to understand that this is my business. I can't pay late the utility bill" grandpa said.
"I think he already know it"
"Mr. Asif thinks I am a weak person."
"hum! This is not right to think that our grandpa has weak personality when two of his relatives are the police office" my brother said to grandpa and then he made his face hard. My brother tried to show that he was supporting our grandpa.

Bumpy road for the grandpa to marry Grandma

Azim and Jamil were laughing loudly. Grandpa and my brother hear it from the living room.
Grandpa changed the topics. And show little distress and worried.
"Moti came last night. Did you see him?" grandpa said slowly.
"yea, I talked with Moti grandpa this morning."
"I saw Azim and Jamil were sitting with him and he was telling the story."
"yea! He was telling them how hard you worked in your life to own four building in the city of Dhaka. And he also talked about your struggle. He was just telling them all those stories. They just want to know about your past." my brother said in a tone that nothing serious was going on.
"I heard Azim and Jamil were laughing loudly."
My brother suppressed his laugh and raised the newspaper to hide him behind the newspaper.
"they usually laugh loudly." my brother said.
"did you ask them what is the reason? Why were they laughing loudly?"
"I told them when people smiles, it is exercise for the muscle of their face. And blood circulates very well in the tissue. And laughing loudly could make them to speak clearly. Good pronunciation. Vocal cord exercised. It is just exercise for the muscle. They are just practicing."

Respond of my brother did not satisfy grandpa. It aggravated his mental distress.
"I need to go to the Bazaar" grandpa said and stood up and left the living room. My brother was looking at him when he was leaving the living room.
After my grandpa left the room, my brother talked himself.
"mercy! Mercy!!"

After ate lunch Moti Grandpa sat down with Azim and Jamil. They were asking him to know about my grandpa. Moti grandpa was very enthusiastic to tell the story of our grandpa.
"grandpa tell us how our grandpa met with our grandma" Azim asked.
"that a long story" Moti Grandpa said.
"tell the story, please grandpa" Jamil request.
"it was month of April. Girl school had annual cultural show. Some girls dance, some girls sing. I, your grandpa and three of your grandpa's friends went to see the cultural show. One girl performed a folklore dance. Then it was turn for your grandma to perform 'doll dance'. She have to dance like a doll."
Jamil and Azim suppressed their laugh. Moti Grandpa looked at them and continued the story.
"would grandma dance like a doll today? we want to see it" Azim said.
"I don't know. You can ask her." Moti grandpa responded.
"did people like it?" Jamil asked.
"oh yea! People was amazed after they saw her to dance like a doll" Moti grandpa responded.
Jamil and Azim tried to laugh but suppress them. Moti grandpa looked at them. He took a pause then he started to tell the story again.
"where did you stop me" Moti grandpa asked himself.

"Oh! You grandpa saw your grandma. She was probably 15/16 years old. It was like a magic. Your grandpa changed. He told me to bring a glass of water. I felt sorry for him. And I bought a glass of water for him."
Jamil and Azim again suppress their laugh. And they were listening the story with good attention. Moti Grandpa again looked at them and continued to tell the story.
"your grandpa became absent minded. He told me to know where

your grandma lived. And I did. Within an hour I collected all the information about your grandma for your grandpa. After that we went home. Your grandpa just lied down in his room. He was not talking that much.
After one day, your grandpa told me "I will marry that girl."
"Which girl I asked." Moti Grandpa said.
 "That girl" your grandpa said.
"Oh! Doll dance girl. I said" Moti grandpa said.
"Your grandpa gave me a hard look at me to show that he did not like what I said 'doll dance girl'. I said 'now what can we do?' he told me to call five of his friends. And I did. We were planning what we could do. Finally we come to the conclusion that first we will propose to the girl's family then we will tell uncle and aunt, your grandpa's parents. Six of us started walking to girl's house. First we were looking for the girl's father. He came out. I do not know how to talk. I said 'we heard you are going to sale rice. I have a rice business.' All your grandpa's friends looked at me surprise. Your grandma's father felt uneasy. He did not understand what the problem is. I told him 'can I have a glass of water?' my mouth was getting dried. Your grandma's father told a boy to bring a glass of water for me. Your grandma's father was a distinguish gentle man. But he was looking at us suspiciously. After that one of your grandpa's friends started talking with your grandma's father. He told your grandma's father that your grandpa was interested to marry your grandma. Bridegroom is the son of the chairman of this union. Your grandma's father did not tell us anything. Only he said that I would think of it. And I need to discuss about it with my other family members."
 We said ok. We left."
Jamil said "what happened?"

Moti grandpa continued "we told your grandpa's father that your grandpa wanted to marry your grandma. He became furious. He wanted first your grandpa to finish the examination. Any way finally we were able to manage him. He agreed to let your grandpa to marry. But your grandma's family did not want your grandpa as their son-in law, because he fought with the people. We tried to manage them. We were able to convince everyone except your grandma's younger brother. He told everyone that no way he would accept your grandpa as his brother-in-law. Your grandpa fought with his friend's older brother for no reason." Jamil and Azim tried to laugh but suppress it.

Moti grandpa continued "one day we found your grandma's brother was at the Bazaar (Hut). He was alone. Your grandpa sent three of his friends to bring your grandma's brother to the office of your grandpa's father. According to the plan of your grandpa, they coaxed him to bring him to the office. After he entered the office, all the doors and windows were shut down. Your grandpa was other room and was observing the situation.

"why am I here?" your grandma's brother asked.

We did not listen to him. We were doing according to the plane we made with your grandpa.

"Why are your shutting the door and the window?" your grandma's brother asked.

We nicely told him to sit down in the office quietly. Your grandpa sent special sweet for your grandma's brother." Jamil and Azim tried to laugh.

Moti Grandpa gave a look to them and continued "we hold him for two hours and tried to manage him and let him to understand that what he thought about your grandpa actually he was not such a kind of person. He was not a fighter at all. He only fought for defense. There was nothing wrong to fight for self-defense.

Moti grandpa took a pause and continued "Indeed your grandpa fought. So we could not deny. Only option was remain for us to explain to him that he only fought for self-defense. He tried to get out from the office. We said to him nicely that it was not time for him to leave the office. Your grandpa told us to be nice with him. He tried to get out from the office. We hold him at the office by keep holding his hand.

"Ok I am not leaving the office. At least release my hands. Would you please release my hands?" your grandma's brother said angrily.

We released his hands. We tried to talk with him.

"let me sit down here quietly. Can I sit here quietly?" he said again angrily.

Six hours after sitting quietly, he asked for a glass of water. I went out from the office to bring a glass of water for him. I saw your grandpa also came out from the private room. Your grandpa gave me two green coconuts for him. I took the green coconut inside the office. I said that your grandpa sent these green coconuts for him. He became furious. It looked to me I drop water in the hot oil. Any way I am trying to make long story short." Azim and Jamil tried to suppress their laugh.

Moti grandpa continued "your grandma's family finally agreed to let to marry your grandpa to your grandma."
"After marry your grandma, your grandpa admitted that it was not a wise plan to keep holding his brother-in-law at his father's office" Moti grandpa said.
Jamil and Azim run away from the room with joy. It was like they found the treasure what they were looking for from Moti grandpa. Moti grandpa went in deep thought.
He was talking himself "I should not tell this story to Jamil and Azim."
He was kind of repenting himself.

Azim and jamil already told everyone about this story. They found me at the corridor in the noon time. They told me in little whispering voice "Montu Bhai, grandpa kidnapped his brother-in-law and forced him to be agree to let his sister to marry our grandpa. They totally deny grandpa. Because grandpa used to fight with the people."
  Grandpa was coming from outside and at the corridor he listen what Azim and Jamil told me. That caused him little mental distress. He looked at us with annoying. But did not tell us anything. He went to his room. Grandma was preparing the bed. At the room, he took off his Panjabi and slightly slamed it at the chair. He was in little distress.
"it was mistake to ask Moti to visit me" grandpa said.
"why did you not think all of these could happen before you kidnap my brother? Now people are laughing at you. My brother Raja is a deputy police commissioner. He can just bring police to arrest you and keep holding you in the police station." grandma said.
She was arguing with grandpa to depend for the Moti grandpa. Also for Azim and Jamil. Grandpa think Azim and Jamil were kind of enemy to him. They are always looking for his fault. And laugh unnecessarily loudly. Grandma always have to depend for them.
"I did not kidnap your brother. I just hold him at dad's office. I offered him sweet, green coconut water." grandpa said.
"he did not even touch your sweet, green coconut water." grandma said in little mockingly.
"if no one want to eat, we can't force them to eat" grandpa said.
"time for you to take a nap as your younger daughter make a routine for you" grandma said with smile and turn her face other side that grandma can't see her face. Grandpa went to take a nap.

He Is My Mother's Father --☺ Anwar Al-Haqq

Grandma left the room.

In the nap he started dreaming that his brother-in-law bought a police force to arrest him. A van load with polices were stop at his gate. Deputy Police commissioner car was ahead of the Van. Deputy Police Commissioner Raj came out from the car.
He ordered the police "go and arrest Rahamat Ullah."
Within a second, the polices came out from the van and rush to arrest Rahmat Ullah from his home. They bring him out from the house with hands were tided at the back with a hand's cuff.
At the gate, Commissioner Raj ordered the Police "take off the hand's cuff. Let him to walk to the van. And take him to the police station."
The police followed the command. Deputy Commissioner's car started moving. The van was following his car and stop behind his car at the Police station.
Deputy Commissioner Raj "take him inside the police station. And hold him in the Lock-up room".
Other police did it instantly. Rahamat Ullah was standing at the lock-up room, the room where the criminal is usually held up before to take to the jail. A police man bought an easy chair and a newspaper for Rahamat Ullah. He sat comfortable on the chair and was reading the newspaper. After that the police man bought tea and cookie for Rahamat Ullah. He drunk tea and eat cookie. One time he lowered the newspaper and looked over it and saw that Deputy Commissioner Raj put his both hands on his back and was walking comfortably to and pro in front of the Lock-up room.
Grandpa wake up from the nap and sat down. He was sweating.
He was talking himself with smile "Raj always is respectful to me. He can't do that".
He took a pause. His mood change again.
"it was mistake to tell Moti to come to my house" grandpa said.
 He took his Panjabi, put on and left the room. He was angrily walking at the corridor and was talking himself. My mom saw that and rushed to come to the corridor with worrying. But grandpa already left the building. Azim and Jamil were observing the situation.
"what happened to my dad" my mom said.
Azim and Jamil came to the corridor.
"aunty. Moti grandpa told the story that grandpa kidnap his brother-in-law. Grandpa thinks it was not appropriate to tell the kidnapping

story. I asked Moti grnadpa "did our grandpa really do it? Moti grandpa nodded his head to say "yes""" Jamil told my mom with little somber and nodded his head to show how Moti grandpa nodded his head.
My mom just gave a little smile to them and said "why does Moti uncle bring all these old stories?".
After that my mom left the corridor and went to her room. I came to the corridor. I saw grandma at the corridor.
  "why not grandpa beat Azim and Jamil" I asked grandma.
"ask your grandpa" grandma respond.
"one time his son just slap in Azim's face. Your grandpa's face become gloomy.
Next morning he called his son and told him "you can discipline him in my absence. Don't do it in front of me."

Azim was Borrowing

Next morning grandpa was reading the newspaper at the shop. His face was behind the newspaper. Azim went to the store and looked at grandpa and took 5 chocolates. Grandpa lowered his newspaper to watch what he was doing, but also do not let Azim to know it. He pretended that he did not see anything. Azim also looked at grandpa that he could not know that he was taking chocolate from the store. Azim already put the chocolate at his pocket. The shopkeeper took a note and tried to give it Azim. Azim gave him the sign that other time. Grandpa lowered his newspaper. He saw the note book.
"hi grandpa" Azim   said.
Grandpa did not respond, but pretend that he was reading something interesting in the newspaper. Azim left. Grandpa told the shopkeeper by pointing to the note book "what is this? Can I see?" Shopkeeper gave the note book to the grandpa. Grandpa opened it. He gave a surprise look. Then he tried to read it carefully. He was reading note little loudly.
"15/03"
Then he looked at the newspaper and looked for the date. "13/12" Grandpa took a pause.
"he is eating food from my store on credit for last one years and 8 months." grandpa talked himself with surprise while he was looking at the note.
"who gave him the permission to buy food from store on credit" grandpa asked the shopkeeper.

Shopkeeper did not respond. He was just listening to grandpa. Grandpa looked at the note again with surprise.
"did he pay any money so far" grandpa asked the shopkeeper. Shopkeeper showed that he become little afraid to answer the question. He just said "no".
"Did you ask for money?"
"no"
"you continue gave him credit to buy from my store".
The shopkeeper remained silent. Grandpa was looking at the note with very interest. And he was reading it.
"15/03 at 10 o'clock in the morning.
4 chocolate: 6 Taka."

"15/03 5 o'clock in the evening.
1 Pepsi: 10 Taka (bottle was return. no deposit for the Pepsi bottle)"
Grandpa was looking at the Note randomly.

"chocolate"
"chocolate"
"Here also 'chocolate'"
"How many chocolate he ate a day. If he eats that many chocolate, there will no teeth left in his mouth."
Grandpa turned the page and said by pointing to the note "here! Here is also chocolate".

"cookie, cookie, Pepsi, Pepsi, Chocolate".
Grandpa stand up and become little serious.
"Do you want me not to sale anything to Azim on credit?" shop keeper asked grandpa.
Grandpa did not respond and pretend that he did not hear anything. Grandpa took the note and walked to the apartment. In the living room Azim was sitting comfortably next to grandma and was reading the newspaper at the easy chair where grandpa usually sit down. Grandma was sewing the pajama of grandpa. Grandpa entered the living room. His face became even more serious. He looked at Azim.
"you! Who gave you permission to buy food from my store on credit?" grandpa asked Azim seriously.
"you were not at the store to asked you to get your permission." Azim respond.
Grandma became little bewilder.

He Is My Mother's Father -- ☺ Anwar Al-Haqq

"what happened?" grandma asked grandpa. She became little serious.
Grandpa gave the note to grandma.
"look at it" grandpa said to grandma.
"what is it? Grandma asked
"look at it. Then you will understand what your grandson did." grandpa said.
Grandma looking at it. And started reading.
"15/03
Chocolate 6 Taka
15/03
Pepsi: 10 Taka"
"What is it" grandma asked grandpa.
"you grandson buying food from my store on credit. He did not even feel to get my permission" grandpa said.
Grandma gave a looked at the note and looked to Azim and smile.
"did you do that?"
Azim node his head to say that yes he did.
"come on here" grandpa asked Azim by pointing to the floor. Azim follow grandpa command and little smile was in his face.
"when are going to give me my money back?" grandpa asked.
"when people do not have job and money, then they borrow money and buy food on credit. After they get the job, then they have money and pay the money back."
"when are you going to get a job?"
Grandpa did not wait for the answer.
"open your mouth" grandpa said.
Azim open him mouth.
"say Ha and open widely"
Azim open mouth widely. Grandpa looked at his teeth very carefully. At that time kids voice were coming from the street "Monkey man! Monkey man!!". It was kind of joyous and cheers for the kids on the street. Azim closed his mouth. "hae!hae!!hae!! Monkey man is here" Azim said loudly and run to go to the balcony.
Grandpa was in the position to examine the teeth of Azim for a while. He was in position to examine the teeth of Azim, but Azim was not there. After that he stood up with little disappointment that he did not get enough time to examine the teeth of Azim.

Monkey Game

Moti grandpa, Azam, Jamil also rushed to come to the balcony. Azim follow them. Grandpa stood for a while to show that he did not finish with Azim yet but he left. Everyone wants to see the monkey's game. Even Azam was busy in his study, he also came to see the monkey game. When grandma saw Azam, she told him to stand in an open space like balcony for a while. She thinks her grandson was studying too hard and sometime smoke come out from his brain. Standing in an open and cool place could cool down his brain. Street could be seen clearly from the balcony. A middle age man and two monkeys were surrounded by kids and with a few middle age and young man. One monkey was small and has the female dress. And one monkey was big compare to the other monkey and had male dress. Monkey's game did not start yet. Monkey man was preparing for it. He was telling the people to move little further to make a room for the monkeys and for him to show the Monkey's game.

After a while, grandma and grandpa also came to the balcony to watch monkey's play. Grandpa went close to Azam and put his right forearm on the shoulder of Azam and looking at the street over the shoulder of Azam. Azam was supporting the weight of grandpa. Grandpa showed that he was very eager to watch the monkey's play. Azim tried to get grandpa's attention.
"if anyone want, he can borrow my shoulder" Azim said for grandpa while he was looking to the street at the monkey.
Grandpa gave a look to Azim with little annoyed and did not show interest to Azim. And he showed that he was comfortable to lean on Azam shoulder.
Moti Grandpa looked at grandma and talked softly "what wrong with Azim shoulder?"
"enemy! Stay with the principle. Don't borrow the shoulder of the enemy." grandma talked little loudly.
Grandpa's eyes were on the street. He did not pay attention to grandma. He showed that he would enjoy the monkey's game. He was waiting curiously when it would start.
"Oh" Moti grandpa said.
"I tried to let him to borrow my shoulder that he will not ask money from me" Azim told grandma.
Grandma smile and looked at Azim.
"you do not have to pay back to your grandpa" grandma said.
Grandpa looked at Grandma then again look at the street.
"if anyone want, he can borrow my shoulder too" Jamil said.

Grandpa also gave a quick look to Jamil with little annoying then looks at the street to watch the monkey's play. Monkey Game started. Monkey man was giving the instruction to the monkeys, and monkey was following the instruction as it was trained.
Monkey man "show them if your girlfriend would be attacked by other monkey, what will you do?"
Male monkey shown that would take a stick and would attack back.
Monkey man "jump over my stick"
Monkey jumped over the stick.
"walked hand on hand with your girlfriend".
Male monkey grab the hand of the female monkey and walked a circle.
"if your wife become sick, what would you do?"
Monkey showed he would take her in his lap and would take care of her.
After a while monkey game was over. Moti grandpa went to the guest room and took his beg and came to the living room where my grandparents were sitting down. He came to tell them good-bye.
"we will go to Noakhali after two days" grandma said.
"see you then. I will go home. After that I will go Noakhali today" Moti grandpa said and left the living room.
Grandma followed him to the stair.
"Moti Bhai" grandma called him from the back.
Moti grandpa stood up and were waiting for grandma. Grandma walked to come close to him.
"don't mind about your Rahmat Bhai's comments. You are always well come to our home" grandma said.
"I know. It was happened in the past and it would happened in the future. This time when he will come to Noakhali, I will catch a big fish from the pond and roast a young chicken for him. When he would see the fish curry and roasted young chicken in his dinner plate, he will forget everything. I have to go."
My grandma smile and said "he says that he don't like you, but when he is in trouble, then only Moti! Moti!!."
"I know" Moti grandpa said and rush to go home.
Grandma went to the living room. Grandpa stood up from the easy chair. "let see what have in the market" grandpa said and went to the market to buy vegetable, fish and meat. In his retire my still he enjoys to go to the market and buy food for the family.

A Jealous Person

He Is My Mother's Father --☺   Anwar Al-Haqq

After one and a half hours, grandpa came back from the market. The boy help us for the house hold job was carrying the beg which is full of vegetable, fish and the meat.
"take the beg to the kitchen and separated the fish. It is on the bottom of the beg." grandpa told the boy. My grandpa use jute made beg for shopping which is 2 feet length and one and half feet wide. So it is a pretty big beg.
"ok" boy said.
Azim heard what grandpa said. He was in the living room. He showed that he was making a quick plan. And he took the plan. He was comfortable sitting in the easy chair of the grandpa and reading the newspaper. And he tried to sit even more comfortably. My mother also was walking toward the living room. Grandma was cleaning the dust of the living room. Grandpa entered the living room. Grandpa eyes were on Azim while he was walking to be close to grandma. Azim did not pay attention to the grandpa. He was in deep concentration to read the newspaper. My mother entered the living room.
""I need to grab his ears and pull it then I should say "get out from my chair"" grandpa said while he was looking to Azim.
Grandma stop the cleaning. Azim moved to sit even more comfortably. Grandpa probably did not realize that my mother entered the living room. Grandpa eyes still were on Azim.
"you are expert to say people 'get out'. You can buy another easy chair for Azim. But that you will not do." grandma said.
Grandpa eyes were still on Azim. Looking at him to see how comfortably Azim was sitting in his chair. His eyes were saying how pleasure for him to see Azim was imitating him.
"does he have the same status as I have?" grandpa said.
My mother was smiling.
"when he sit at that chair and read the newspaper, I feel like my dad is sitting on the chair." my mother said.
Grandpa took his eye off from Azim.
"don't call Azim as your Dad in front of your father. His tummy is full of jealousy." grandma told my mother.
Grandma took a pause and said "I paid the tuition fee."
My mother smile and left the living room.

Grandpa Like to give the gift to his grandchildren

Next morning Azim and Jamil went to their school with my aunts.

They went to the school to get the result of their final exam. They did well in the exam. They happily came back home. They showed their Progress Report (PR) to every one of the home except grandpa who went to the market to buy the grocery. They gave their PR to me. I gave them congratulation to do well in the exam. They gave it to grandma. She looked at it for a while. She also looked very happy and gave them a hug. Grandpa came from the market with the boy who helped us to do our household job. After came from the market, grandpa went to his bedroom.
"go! Show your PR to your grandpa." grandma told Azim and Jamil. Grandma, Azim and Jamil walked to the bed room of my grandparents.
"give your PR to your grandpa" grandma told again Azim and Jamil at their bedroom.
They walked close to grandpa and gave their PR to him. He was looking it very carefully and smile was in his face. He was amazed to see PR. Then suddenly his face became serious. He was pointing in the PR. One time to the Azim's PR and other time to Jamil's PR. They became little bewilder. They looked at grandma to get her attention. But grandma was still smiling.
"problem is here! And here!!" grandpa pointed to both PR.
"score in Bengali and in English. 100 was the total point. You two even did not come close to it. Even not close to 95." grandpa said. Azim and Jamil faces became little dry and were watching grandpa.
"I told you two to study hard. Take it" grandpa said and gave back the PR to them.
"nothing will make you happy" Azim told with somber.
Grandma tried to share their feeling. They went out from my grandparents room. In the evening, grandpa went to the sweet soap and bought five killo-Gram of sweet for the family. He also bought the Story Books for Azim and Jamil.

At the evening, Azim and Jamil were at the TV room. They passed the examination. No one was disciplining them. They got more freedom that night. They were watching TV. It had 220 channels. Jamil press the button of the TV. A channel came. It was showing American Hollywood movie. They were watching in the middle of it, but somehow both Azim and Jamil liked it. At the middle of the movie, it was shown that there was a castle. After that it showed that there was a backyard inside the castle. The backyard was enclosed by the high wall of the castle. There were 30 kids about

He Is My Mother's Father -- ☺ Anwar Al-Haqq

5/6 years old. They were divided in two groups. One group had red dress and red cap. Red shirt had white belt and plain red paint. And cap had white ribbon. Other group had blue dress and blue hat and same white belt at the shirt and white ribbon at the cap. They were standing in three rows in each group. Red dressed kids were one side and blue dressed kids were other side. Two 50/60 years old ladies were standing at the both end. Each kid had a sword which was hanging at their right side near to their belt. A shield was also on their right hand. The ladies were on same dressed as the kids, but did not have sword and shield. The ladies dressed like a queen. They had a crown on their head. When they walked or run, one lady was at the front and other lady was at the back. She was the last person. One time it showed that they were running slowly. The lady was at the back: her hands were moving left to right while she was running. Hands were in bending position and tense. While she was running, she became almost the size of the kids. The lady was at the front was running in more relaxing condition. Front lady came close to the wall. There was no room for her to move forward. Suddenly she said loudly "Attttttttaaaack (attack)!"

Everyone turned back. The kids were in her group put their left hand on the handle of the sword instantly. But they did not take the sword out from it sheath. The lady was at front now running behind of everyone. The lady at the back became tense and also became almost the size of the kids. As she was running, she was getting back to normal and at normal size. While the kids were running, their head were little forward then their feet. They were well disciple and marching. After a while, their left hand went back to previous position. Now the front lady came close to the wall. She suddenly said loudly "Attttttttttttttaaaaack"

Everyone turned back and stared running. They did the same thing two times. Suddenly message came "You are watching the full length Movie: *THE LAZY ARMY.* You will watch the rest of the movie after the commercial break."

I saw this Movie long ago. It was a story about two princes in Europe. After the sudden death of their father they tried to become the queen of the country. Administration split in half and continue quarrel was going on at the Kingdom. And people were suffering. Finally people revolt against them and through them out from power and just gave them this castle. They open a school inside the castle. Still they have some supporter and they are loyal to them. Their kids study on that school. Now younger sister become respectful to the older sister. They were using the undoing mechanism and want to go back to their past as royal family. But both sisters have mental problem after they lost the power. Sometime they tried to do what they supposed to do as a princess. Sometime they blame the army not to fight for them against the country man to keep them on power. Anyway the movie tried to tell the people that suddenly don't try to change the system of an institute, it may cause greater harm to the people those who live under that institution such as like in this story the younger sister struggled to be the queen and their country people were suffering and after that they themselves also were suffering.

Anyway during the commercial break, Jamil change the channel. In the next channel it was shown that a man slided his right hand on the air over his left hand. Hands did not touch each other. He made a sound. Then he showed hold his right hand in the air. Then he use his both hands. Then he made the sound. Then he shown that he grab something and threw. Then he use one hand on top of other. Then he constantly bringing his right hand close to the mouth. Then the person asked the audience. What I did?
One audience said "you made a cup of tea."
"correct" the actor said.
Sound came from TV " you are watching the show: *TELL ME*".

Be Patient

I was walking through the TV room. I just gave a look at the TV room. Azim saw me.
"Rontu Bhaya" Azim said.
I respond.
"look! Grandpa bought story book for us. One for me and other for Jamil." Jamil said.
They looked very happy to get gift from the grandpa. Azim gave me the hand sign and said "come and look".
I went to them. They were very eager to show me their story book. I took the story books in my hand.
"definitely grandpa bought good story books for two of you" I said.
I showed them that I was happy to see the books.
"I read two stories. It had total 10 stories" Jamil said.
"it had beautiful story." Jamil added.
"Rontu Bhaya! Sit here. I will read a story for you. It is very

beautiful." Azim said.
"I have to go. My friends are waiting for me" I said.
"Just one stories. please" Azim said.
Against my will, I sat to listen the stories. Azim started to tell the stories.
"There was a prince. One day he went out to see his father's kingdom. He had 50 companions with him. He was on the horse. They came to a plain land next to the sea and on the valley of the hill. They stop on their. A little distance from them, they saw a girl with well dress was sitting in an easy chair. Six female were taking care of her, and also carrying her order. 60 soldiers were guarding her.
"your majesty! we are at the end of the border of our kingdom" one old man who is also the assistant to the Prince said to the Prince.
"You want us not to move forward?" prince said.
"yes! Your majesty. If we proceed, war will break out" assistant to the prince said.
"hold on" prince said.
Everyone stood up.
"who are those people on the sea beach?" Prince asked his assistant.
"Your majesty! could be the member of the Royal family. Proceeding further could provoke them to engage in war. We lost these lands to them in last battle. Still we are trying recovering from the loose of the last battle. It was a catastrophe for our force. They lost their courage."
"why I don't know it" prince asked.
"your majesty! you were a just 2 years old. King decided only to tell you his success. Good news is that our king's rival does not have a son. And daughter could not be the queen and to be the head of the kingdom. We are just waiting for this opportunity. The turmoil. " the assistant respond.
"what about son-in-law?" Prince asked.
"your majesty! kingdom constitution does not have bar for the son-in-law to be the king. But king's three nephews are the candidate to be the king. Turmoil could be happened to select the heir for the thrown after the death of the king. They don't marry a close relative." assistant said.
"what is the legal marriage age at our rival kingdom?"
"Your majesty. 18 for both boy and girl"
"how old is the princess?"

"Your majesty! 20 years old. Two years younger than our prince"
"can I send a messenger to them that I am the prince who want to meet with the royal family members of my neighbor?" Prince asked.
"your majesty! You can. But our king was denied several times before. When our army does n't match with the power of their army, we tried to negotiate with them to get our land back, but denied" assistant said to the prince.
"The chief of the army is very kind and generous to the people but at the battle field he is very ruthless. And he is a very skill full general and loyal to the king. He trained a disciplined army for the king" the assistant added.
"send a messenger to the Royal family member" prince ordered.
"yes! Your majesty. Letter has to be written in more polite way." assistant respond.
The messenger was sent to the neighbor's Royal family member. The messenger was guided to take to the princess. The messenger read the message of the Princess "I am the prince of the Tangland have the message to the Honorable Princess of the Amriland. I am requesting to get permission to meet with the princess. I hope the princess would not deny my request"
"you prince is invited to meet with me" Princess respond to the message.
The messenger showed the respect to the princess. And the messenger left.

The messenger came back with the good news. The princess, the only daughter of king, wants to meet with the prince. Surge of happiness run over the side of the prince camp.
"you majesty! Many thank to god. I was worried that she would deny your request. If her father would know it, he would scold her for sure. But our spy gave us the report that king love his daughter very much" assistant said to prince.
"so why are we standing here? Move on" prince ordered.
When the prince reached the border of the other kingdom, he was given a warm welcome and was taken to the princess. Princess fall in love to the prince at their first meeting. After the meeting with the princess, Prince came back to his place. After one month, King, and prince were invited. King became very happy.
"why she took a month to invite us?" prince asked his assistant.
"your majesty. Our spy said that King was denying princess request for last one month. Finally king melt down" assistant respond.

"good. Do you think the rivalry also will disappear?" prince asked.
"your majesty! I am optimistic. The princess did not realize that her maid is our spy. Our spy became her trusted maid. The Princess told everything to our spy that how much she our love prince." assistant respond.
"our spy was well trained" prince said.
"your majesty! Spies are trained under my supervision and my instruction" assistant said.
"good! This box is full of gold and diamond. This is for you as a reward."
"thank you. Your honor. Your servant is ready to carry on his duty to satisfy his master." assistant showed his respect to the princes.
The King and the prince went to visit the neighboring kingdom.
Prince married the princes.
"this is the end of the story" Azim said.
"thank you" I said
"you want me to read an another story. This one is better than this one. You would love it" Azim said.
"no! no!! thank you. I have to go. Friends are waiting for me. I wish you will get a princess like this prince. And also will able to double the size or triple the size of your property like this prince." I said and stool up. I showed them that I am rush to meet my friends.
"Jamil when I will come back I will also listen your story." I said both Jamil and Azim and I left to meet my friends. On the way to go to meet with my friend I was thinking: Jamil probably would be tell me a story of prince who waited for the princess for 1000 years. After that it came to my mind "if Azim could act as a prince and our Moti grandpa would act as an assistant to the prince how it would be like". While I was thinking all of these suddenly it came in my mind that one day grandpa was reading the Bangla translation of Koran and it said "be patients, if you think you are belong to the group of the believer". Grandpa explain to me that God want people to be patients whatever the hardship come to them as a test. And at that situation should remain faithful to God. He is the one who could take out the people from the hardship. And people should show the satisfaction to the God decision. This is the way a person could please God. All the prophets (PBUT) of Allah went through the hardship. And they remain faithful to God and they submit their will to God during their hardship. This king was not on hardship but he was patients.

At night, Azim lied down at sofa and was reading a story book. While reading the story book, he fall sleep on the sofa. My uncle and my aunt, Azim's Mother, came to take him to the bed.
"after a whole day fighting with the grandpa, now fell in sleep" my uncle said.
"why not his grandpa grab his nose to break it to annoying him" my aunt said.
"His grandma is on his side. He has the confidence that grandpa would not do anything" uncle said.
My uncle took Azim from the sofa to his right shoulder and aunt was walking behind to take him to the bed.

Visiting Noakhali

Next morning grandpa, grandma, Azim and Jamil were preparing to go to Noakhali. Driver bought the car and parked in front of the building. Driver was sitting inside the car. Grandpa bought this Toyota Corolla 5 year ago. Usually grandpa did not use the cane to get support while he walked. He brought the cane long ago. Occasionally, he uses it when he went out with grandma, Azim and Jamil. That morning he was carrying the cane to walk around. Cane was not supporting him, but he was carrying the cane. My both aunts were at the balcony to watch the car and their departure. They were talking. Azim and Jamil were helping grandma to load two begs at the car's tank. Grandma went to the back seat of the car. She sat middle of the back seat. Jamil sat left side of grandma. Azim sat in the front seat. He sat very comfortably.
"look at Azim, he Sat liked my dad" Aunt, Jamil mum, told to Azim's mother.
Aunt, Azim mother, smile and said "wait and see. How long can he sit in the front seat?"
Azim turn his neck to the back and tried to talk with grandma. Grandpa was walking toward the car.
"come here" grandma said to Azim.
Azim did not pay attention to her and start talking "Noakhali is famous for its green coconut."
Grandpa stood next to Azim. He stood there for a while. He saw Azim was not paying attention. Azim was talking with grandma.
 "I must ···"
Before Azim finished his sentence, grandpa put his cane through the

window of the car and knocked Azim. Azim startled. He looked at grandpa then he looked at grandma.
His physical gesture was shown to grandma that he did not understand the justification of the action of grandpa.
 "why did he knock me? What did I do?" Azim asked grandma.
Grandpa was standing with a serious mood next to the front seat of the car.
"This is your grandpa's car. Did he not tell you before?" Grandma said.
"I bought this car" grandma added what grandpa told before. Grandma took a brief pause.
 Then she said "Front seat is only reserve for your grandpa."
"Can't give up the claim of the ownership of the car." grandma said with little sarcastically.
"Come here." grandma told Azim by showing the right side of the back seat of the car.
"as your grandpa said before "this is my mercy to give him a ride to take him to Noakhali "" grandma said.
Grandpa did not pay attention to anyone. Azim went out of the car. And he sat right side of grandma. Grandpa went and sat to the front seat as comfortably as he can. Grandpa gave the feeling that even they were going together in Noakhali, he was not belong to their group. He tried to keep little distance from them. Car started to travel to Noakhali. My aunts were looking at the car as long as they can see the car.

The house my grandpa has in the rural area of Noakhai has six homes. Two homes were belong to our grandpa. And other four were belong to Moti grandpa and his brother. There was a courtyard among those homes.

Next morning, grandpa hired two labors to dig up the soil from the rice field to make a little high ground where he can plant trees. The labor came to dig up the rice field. They bought their lunch, spade and baskets with them. Their lunch was on a plate which was covered and tied up with a cloth. Grandpa came to home. He collected two spades and a basket. He put those in the courtyard of the house. Grandpa used his hand to called Azim and Jamil in come close to him where he kept the spades and the basket.
"come here" grandpa command them. His face was stony hard. Grandpa was talking loudly. Azim and Jamil looked each other face

after that went to grandpa. Moti grandpa was watching the situation curiously from the door of his home. He was sitting in a chair. Grandma was standing at the door of their home.

"take the spade and the basket" grandpa command them.

Azim and Jamil look at each other face again and took the basket and the spades. Grandma showed her sympathy to them.

"follow me" grandpa said.

Azim and Jamil were walking behind grandpa. Grandpa took them to the rice field where the two labors were working.

"help them. And listen them what they would tell you. They are your supervisor. You two do not have experience to dig up the rice field."

Azim and Jamil looked at each other. Then they became enthusiastic to work with the labors. Grandpa was in serious mood. And he left. After a while grandma came to watch them from a distance. She looked with sympathy to them. But Azim and Jamil did not see her. She stood there for a while and watched them that they were working with the labor. They first used the spade to dig up the soil to fill the basket then both were carrying the basket to make a high land.

After a while Moti grandpa was walking through the rice field where Azim and Jamil were working. Moti grandpa stood there for a while. When Azim and Jamil saw Moti grandpa, they stop working and stood up.

"grandpa" Azim said.

Moti grandpa did not show much interested to talk with them at this time.

"how many way your grandpa will save the money?" Moti grandpa said and left with gently shaking his head.

Azim and Jamil remain in standing and were watching that Moti grandpa was walking away from them. They were little surprise that Moti grandpa did not talked with them.

After walked for a little distance from Azim and Jamim, Moti grandpa smile and talked himself "you two still don't know Rahamat Bhai yet. Laugh loudly! Now get the test to laugh at loudly at Rahmat Bhai."

Azim and Jamil remain standing and was looking at Moti grandpa.

"work! Work!! your grandpa told us not to let you to talking with anyone" one labor said.

"you grandpa said "they came to work and they will only work. No talk. Don't stay in standing."" other labor said.

They went back to work. It was around 11 o'clock in the morning. And was lunch time for the labor. Grandpa bought two plates which were covered with a cloth like the labor bought the plate with them. He also bought a Jar which fill with water. He did not bring a cup for them to pour the water on it from the jar. When Azim and Jamil saw it, they looked at each other face.
"lunch for two" grandpa told and gave them and left.
Azim and Jamil looked at each other. They did not understand what grandpa was doing.
They ate lunch with the labors. Grandpa was watching then from a distance. After ate the lunch, the labor went back to work.
"this is time to work" one labor told Jamil and Azim.
Azim and Jamil went back to work. After a while, grandpa came and told the labor "this is enough for today."
Azim and Jamil show little joy. They picked the basket, spades, the plate, jar and the cup. They were walking normally to come home. Grandpa was behind them. He gave a smile then became serous as he was before. After walked for a while, they came to the courtyard of the home. Grandma was using a broom to sweeping the dust of the courtyard of the home. Grandma stood up after she saw them. Just they saw grandma, they show her that they were exhausted by digging up the soil. They went to grandma. Grandma put her hands to their shoulder then gave them a hug same time.
"Oh! You two are exhausted" Grandma showed her sympathy and affection to them.
 "Your grandpa even not hesitated to tell you to dig up the soil. Don't laugh loudly at your grandpa any more" grandma said.
They shake their head that they would not.
"go take the towel and soap, and go to the pond to take shower" grandma told them.
Azim and Jamil took their towel and soap and walked to the pond to take shower. Grandma was watching to them and smiling while they walked to the pond.
"now get the lesion to mess around with the grandpa" grandma talked herself.
Azim and Jamil went to the pond. The pond had a stair to walk into the deep of the pond water. They knew how to swim. Taking shower at the pond was kind of fun for them. They usually spend at least half an hour at the pond, if it was a winter time like the month of December and January. Other time they even spend two/three hours at the pond. There was a tree which was leaning over the

pond. They usually climbed to the tree and jump into the pond from the tree. They showed their different skill while they jumped from the tree. They brought their knees close to their chest and hold it firmly then they free fall from the tree into the pond. After a while grandma came to check what they were doing. It was a winter time. Grandma was concern that if they stayed long time into the pond, they could have a cold. Grandma went to the stair of the pond. She found them into the pond and was swimming. Some time they dived into the bottom of the pond and bring out the clay to show that they could dive up to the bottom of the pond.
"come here" grandma told them.
They followed grandma's instruction and came to the stair. Grandma gave them the towel. They were shivering.
"look at you. You are shivering. You two are still diving into the water. You could get cold. Dry up the body with towel and stand on the here where have the sun" grandma told them. They were listening to grandma.

In the evening, Moti grandpa was sitting on the grass which was close to the stair of the pond. He was reading a book. Azim and Jamil saw him and walked to him. Jamil sat right side and Azim sat left side of Moti grandpa.
"grandpa temper is little hot today" Jamil said.
Moti grandpa smile and said with affection "I also fell the same. This is an old man syndrome. Don't worry. I caught a big fish from the pond today. And I slaughter a young chicken for him. Tonight when he will see that roasted whole young chicken and the fish curry in his dinner plate, his mood will be up. You would see everything is normal for him."
"do you think so?" Azim asked.
"yes I think so" Moti grandpa respond very affectionately.
Our grandpa saw that Moti grandpa was talking with Azim and Jamil. It caused him little distress and suspicious. He called Rafik, the person who take care the properties of our grandpa, Moti grandpa and his brother in their absence.
"just go and sit next to them. Don't tell them anything. Don't tell them that I send you to them. And listen what they were talking about. And tell me word to word after that" grandpa told Rafik in whispering voice.
Rafik walked to the Moti grandpa.
"hi!" Raifk said.

Moti grandpa gave him sing by hand to sit. Rafik sat close to the Moti grandpa. He was listening to them. Sun was set. They went to the home. Grandpa walked to Rafik and asked "what were they talking about?"
"Moti grandpa was telling them the story how hard you worked to raise their parents and the contribution of their grandma in your family." Rafik said.
"are you sure that they were talking about" grandpa asked.
"swear to God ……." Rafik said.
Before Rafik finished his sentence, grandpa said "you do not have to swear to me or to God".
"Ok! You can go." grandpa told Rafik.
Rafiq was about to leave. Grandpa took a pause. Then he said slowly to Rafik "Just don't tell anyone that I sent you to them."
Rakif left. Grandpa because assure and was smiling that Moti grandpa talked about his hard working with his grandsons. He wanted to tell those stories to his grandkids. But he did not find the opportunity to tell those stories to them.

Next morning, grandpa mood was little better, but was not as good as Azim and Jamil were expected. Rafik had two ox, cows which give milk , and few goats. Those Ox were very strong and use to plowing the rice field. One corner of the courtyard, the ox were tied up inside a home. My grandparents, Moti grandpa, Azim and Jamil were sitting on the courtyard. They just finished their breakfast. Rafik took out one ox from it home. He would take all of his livestock to the rice field to let them to graze. Azim stood up and told Rafik "let me take the Ox to the field".
Rafiq gave the rope of the Ox to Azim. The ox became somehow irritated. It first tried to run. Azim hold it strongly but fall on the ground then it drag Azim. Rafik went to hold the rope of the ox. Grandpa was watching the situation first with panic then with curiosity. He raised his right hand. Right elbow was close to his chest. He moved his hand from the back to the front several times. This is kind sign to insult someone. This sign people use to show other that he is nothing. Grandpa tried to let Azim know that he can't even hold the rope of an ox. Azim also showed to grandpa that he was ashamed.
"grandpa" Azim said.
Grandpa did not pay attention to him.
"you want me to take them to the market. If people know it, I would

have no option except to use hajab, a head cover, to go to the market" grandpa told grandma.

"grandpa" Azim said again.

""people will tell me "your grandson even can't handle an ox"" grandpa add.

"don't worry. They will make you proud" grandma said to grandpa. Rafik's son bought out the goat from it home.

"give me the goat" Azim told little loudly in commanding voice to Rafik's son.

Rifik's son gave the goat to Azim. Azim was pulling the goat toward his side. Goat made his feet stiff to make resistance not to come toward Azim. Azim tried to pull gently the goat to take to the field. But goat was resisting. Then he suddenly forcefully pull the goat. Goat came toward him.

"only you can beat the goat" grandpa said to Azim.

Azim looked at grandpa and smile little mockingly. Azim followed Rafik and took the goat to the rice field. Moti grandpa was silent so far. He was listening to them. With little frustration he said "my grandson wrote a big love letter to a girl."

Before Moti grandpa finished his statement, grandpa asked "which one?"

"the one who is a ninth grade student" Moti grandpa respond.

"it is too early to know how to write a love letter. Then what happened?" grandpa said.

"next day that girl bought that love letter to school and told all her friends and use the letter to targeted on my grandson's head. Her friends laugh loudly." Moti grandpa said.

"oooohh! I was suspicious that he did not able to write a good love letter" my grandpa said.

"if I see the girl's grandpa, how would I be able to keep my head straight up?" Moti grandpa said.

"just coax the grandpa and his granddaughter to come to your home. After that tie them under your table" grandpa said.

"you are expert of it. Tie them! Hold them!! And offer them sweet and coconut water" grandma said little sarcastically.

My grandpa was smiling.

"we are proud for our grandpa" Jamil said and tried to lean on grandpa. Grandpa tried to push him away from him. But Jamil came even more closer to grandpa.

Next morning car was waiting at the courtyard of the house for my

grandparents, Azim and Jamil to take them in Dhaka. Moti grandpa came to Noakhali to take care some of his business. He needed to stay few more days at Noakhali. He was standing at the right side of the car. Grandpa walked to the car and sat at the front seat. He did not say anything to Moti grandpa. He looked little serious. Azim and Jamil gave a hug to Moti grandpa and said good bye. My grandma said good bye to Moti grandpa. And they walked to the car.
Grandma sat in the middle. And Azim sat right side and Jamil sat left side of grandma.
"you did not said anything to Moti Bhai" grandma said to grandpa and after that grandma looked at Moti grandpa.
Grandpa even became more serious. Moti grandpa was watching the situation and was smiling. Grandma also smiled with him. And pointed to grandpa. Azim and Jamil were watching the situation. And they were trying to understand the situation.
"Moti Bhai, when you will come to Dhaka, come to visit us" grandma told Moti grandpa.
Grandpa looked back while grandma was talking with Moti grandpa and tried get even more serious. He wants to avoid Moti grandpa. Azim and Jamil were watching grandpa out of curiosity.
"grandpa came to visit us before our school will started" Azim told Moti grandpa.
Grandpa looked at Azim and he showed that he did not like what Azim told Moti grandpa. Car started. It took hundred eighty degree turn.
"grandpa come to visit us" Jamil told Moti grandpa.
Grandpa looked also this time to the back and looked at Jamil and showed his discontent.
"this time bring Babe to our home when you will come to visit us" grandma said to Moti grandpa.
We called brother's wife or brother-in-law's wife 'Babe' instead to call her by name.
Car started to running to its destination, Dhaka. Grandpa got time to relaxed in his car.

After worked hard in his life, now was the time to relax that was his attitude. So everywhere he got the opportunity to sit down, he sit down with relax. He needed a wide space to sit down. Sometime we have to squeeze ourselves as his grandkids to make enough room for him. He needed enough room for his legs at his car. This was his car what he always claimed to his grandsons.

Grandpa as a Judge

This is my grandpa who still love the village where he born and grown up. He also wishes his grave would be at his village. The place he born and the same place he wanted to be buried. The way he visit the grave of his parents and the grandparents and the other relative, his children and grandchildren would visit his grave and ask God to forgive his sin and let him to live in the paradise. And the village people still respect him. Most of the rural (village) people do not know what court is and why need a Judge and lawyer. If the rural people have any dispute to one another, they usually come to the educated people or wealth people or who is influential at the rural area to solve their dispute. Most of the rural people can't effort to go to the town and hire the lawyer to run their case. When my grandpa comes to the village, sometime he has to appear as one of the Judge. In the rural area usually a group of people sit as a Judge and give the court order together. In the US standard, they have the double role: Judge and the Jury. Those who sit as a Judge, most of them be Judge to meet the community demand. They like it or not is not the question here. To live in a community they can't deny the community request. This is also the process to keep the social order at the rural area.   Sometime my grandpa shares his role as a Rural Judge to his friends. Mr. Ansari always questions the qualification and the quality of Judge my grandpa could be. After Mr. Ansari first time heard of that my grandpa also become judge time to time at the rural area, he frowned his forehead and gave a suspicious looked at my grandpa. Mr. Ansari thinks he has the reason to raise the question about the honesty of my grandpa, because grandpa told the story about Moti Grandpa which happened 54 years ago to Mr. Ansari, Mr. Motin and Mr. Jalil. Moti grandpa also fell in love to a girl when he was ninth grade student. But he did not know what to do about his feeling. One day the girl was going home at the evening with two other girls from school. Moti Grandpa pulled the head scarf of the girl. The girl busted out like a flame. Next day the girl told everyone about the incident. She told our grandpa and other to justify his cousin's action. But my grandpa took Moti grandpa's side.
"no way Moti can do it. I know him very well. I know which plate he use to eat food and which bathroom he use to take shower. No way he can do it" my grandpa told the people.

"Everyone looked at me with annoyed" my grandpa said.
There was a witness and they told 'indeed Moti did it".
"After everyone found Moti as Guilty, I become silent" my grandpa said. "after that Moti lost his interest for that flamed girl" my grandpa added.
At the end of the story, Mr. Ansari came close to grandpa and whispered to my grandpa "You just took the side of your cousin. Did you?"
My grandpa shocked his head for the approval. Mr. Ansari gave a suspicious look at my grandpa. My grandpa gave a look back to Mr. Ansari and was thinking for a while "I should not tell this story".
Mr. Ansari told my grandpa what Allah said in Koran in his words "when you will sit to judge, judge fairly. If the judgment even goes against your family member, don't hesitate to declare them that they are the guilty one. Or God will judge the people in the Day of Judgment. He will not do any injustice to anyone at that day. God commanded people to establish justice." Mr. Ansari gave an example. If son did injustice to someone and parents tried to hide it, parents also did the injustice to the victim. In this case actually parents spoiled the future of their son because they act against the rules of God. When people act against the Rules of God, people are in trouble. This trouble could occur in this world or at the hereafter or both places. Mr. Ansari said "God knows what we reveal to the people and what we hide."
Anyway even Mr. Ansari has the question about the honesty of my grandpa, Mr. Matin most of the time agree with my grandpa and considered that it was the proper judgment. Sometime Mr. Ansari also agree with my grandpa. Give an example. One day a young man after two years of his marriage beat his wife. And the wife complained to my grandpa. Grandpa ordered the young man to ask for apology to his wife and buy a new cloth for her. This was the Judge order. So the young man followed the Judge order. Mr. Ansari and Mr. Matin support my grandpa. Both agreed that the man also need to respect their wife. Because the women are weak compare to man physically and they depend on bread and butter to their husband in the rural area, they should not be subject of physical torture. Woman also take care the family. They do the household job. On return they do not ask for money.

This is my grandpa who is also a judge. Give another example. One day two farmers fought at the Bazaar. They were sharing the bull to plow the land. Each of them had only one bull. But two bulls are needed to plow the land. One of the farmer lives close to my grandpa and he was not physically that strong. And his son work in Dhaka as a labor. Another farmer lives one mile away from my grandpa's house. The farmer who used to live one mile away from my grandpa's house had an argument with the farmer who lived close to my grandpa's house. From the argument, strong farmer started fighting and beat badly the weak farmer. Both farmers were waiting for my grandpa to solve the problem. Weak farmer's son wants to take the revenge. After a week of the fight, my grandpa went to the rural area. The strong farmer met with my grandpa at the bazaar at night. My grandpa just listen the story without giving any opinion. Next morning my grandpa called the weak farmer to his house and also listen his story. Then he asked two other people about the incidence. My grandpa found more inconsistency in the story of the strong farmer then the weak farmer. Without doing anything, my grandpa just left the rural area. And he came to Dhaka. He called the son of the weak farmer to his house. And made a plot to beat him the way the strong farmer beat the weak farmer. Strong farmer would able to take more blow. So it was decision that he would beat more than he beat the weak farmer. My grandpa called the strong farmer to plow one of his paddy land. Strong farmer with hesitation agree to plow my grandpa's paddy land. He can't just deny the request of my grandpa. In the morning, the strong farmer came to plow that paddy land. Instead of plowing the land, he was beaten by the people of the weak farmer. Weak farmer was so mad to take the revenge that he used a branch of tree to beat him which has the throng on it. Then the weak farmer spread the Hot Paprika power on him. Other people did not let it to go any further. They stop the beating. The strong farmer jumped at the pond to cool down. My grandpa became mad to hear the story of the beating process. He considered excessive force was applied and also little brutality, using the Paprika. Now he sat with other rural people to solve the people. They fined 200 US dollar equivalent Bangladeshi currency to the weak farmer which my grandpa gave him as a donation after two weeks. After that we did not here any problem exist between these two farmers.

One day grandpa told about this story to Mr. Ansari. Mr. Ansari jumped up to hear the story.
"It was not a fair judgment. You can't not change the criterion of the

Judgment. Poor or rich. Weak or strong. All are equal to the justice system of Islam. " Mr. Ansari told.

My grandpa's mouth became dry and his face became little gloomy. "What was wrong in my judgment?" grandpa asked with mumbling voice.

"You just need to hear case from two side and from the witness. And after that you have to find anyone was guilty or not like in this case was the strong farmer. You had to give the weak farmer the choice. Does he want to beat the strong farmer the way he beat him or weak farmer can choose to get the compensation?" Mr. Ansari said.

After took a pause, Mr. Ansari said "you did the serious mistake."

"What was it?" my grandpa said with weak voice.

"You told the strong farmer to work in your farmland and let the weak farmer to beat him. Allah knew very well what your intension was. You just took the advantage of your position in the society. Remember that Allah has the power over everything. You high social status is the test from Allah that you would not abuse your power out of fear of Allah. This was a kind of deception even you did not realized. Deception and hypocrisy are the worse kind of sin in Islam."

Grandpa asked with tearing eyes "now what should I do?"

"You need to ask sincerely to Allah for forgiveness and also at the same you need to ask for forgiveness from the strong farmer. You need to make the strong farmer happy. Remember that Allah does not love those who are arrogant. Satan was outcaste due to his arrogant behavior." Mr. Ansari said.

Grandpa became bewildered and asked with little panic "What should I do?"

"I already told you. Go to the village and ask for the forgiveness from the strong farmer. Strong farmer is stronger than the weak farmer, you are strong than the strong farmer, and Allah has the power over everyone. Allah is severe in punishment. And Allah is most merciful to his obedient slave, the human being. " Mr. Ansari said.

Next morning grandpa went to the village. In the evening, he reached to his village's house. And staying overnight to his village's house. Next morning after the dawn prayer, grandpa went to the house of the strong farmer himself. Strong farmer after the dawn prayer lied down lazily to take a rest before go to the farmland to work.

Grandpa called by name the strong farmer with little sad voice but loudly.
Strong farmer hear his name and did not give the important.
Grandpa called his name again after a while.
"Is not our brother Rahmat?" strong farmer raises his head from the bed and asked his wife.
Grandpa called him again. Strong farmer rushed to come to meet with grandpa without getting respond from his wife.
"you are in a poor man house. If you tell someone to let me know to meet with you, I would be at your home." Strong farmer said.
Tear was in the eyes of my grandpa. Strong farmer became nervous and asked "what did happen brother Rahmat?"
"I commit a serious sin. And only you can help me to get rid of this sin." Grandpa said somberly.
"What are you talking about?" strong farmer said with little crying voice.
"Because of me Ali got the opportunity to torture you. What I did was a kind of deception." Grandpa said with weak voice. Ali was the name of the weak farmer.
"You do not have to ask for forgiveness. You are one of the respected person in our society." Strong farmer said.
"my position in the society does not have any value to Allah. Allah gave us the guidance, the Koran. Did we follow it or not would be matter to Allah." Grandpa said.
Strong farmer became mute. And looked at grandpa.
Grandpa hold the hand of the strong farmer and said "would you forgive me."
"If I said that I forgive you and you would be happy, I forgive you." Strong farmer said.
"you need to forgive me with open mind. Without keeping any discontent in your mind" Grandpa hold the hand of the strong farmer.
"I forgive you with my open mind." Strong farmer said.
Grandpa gave the strong farmer a hug. After gave the hug, grandpa said "this world is nothing but delusion. Hereafter will be permanent. Those who would enter the paradise will be the successful one. You will see a lot of powerful kings will be drag into the hell fire and a lot of weak people will go to the paradise. Same way a lot of king will go to the paradise and a lot of weak people

will be drag into the hell fire. Those who would fear God in this world will be the successful one."
Strong farmer was listening my grandpa with little bewildering and ask "who told you that you were wrong?"
"Mr. Ansari." My good friend.
"My heart also constantly telling me that you deceived me. But today I do not have pain I bear after that incident. Allah is all forgiver. So am I." strong farmer said.
"Tear of your eyes also made my eyes tearful and wipe away my all the pain and the anger I had to you. Even yesterday my heart was seeking to take the revenge. But I was weak to take the revenge. The pain I bear after that incidence was seeking for the revenge. I was telling myself that Allah is with those who has the patient. And I tried to find the consolation on it. And at the same time I was seeking Allah to judge for it. Because I do not know what would be the outcome."
"I am sorry." My grandpa cry out.
"Allah would let me to go through the pain as like you. It would be multiply and long." My grandpa said with crying voice.
"I forgive you and may Allah also forgive you." Strong farmer said. Strong farmer gave a hug to grandpa and said "you friend is a real Muslim. I wish I can give him a hug."
"Off course you can give him a hug. He is a good man. And a good Muslim. You can go with me to Dhaka to meet with him and be my guest." Grandpa said.
"Today I have a confidence that I would be not neglected by you because I am poor." Strong farmer said.
"I will be happy to meet Mr. Ansari."
"I am also see the change on you." My grandpa said.
"I talked with the Imam of the Mosque and I told him my intention to take the revenge. Imam help me to deal with this pain. I was restless. From that situation, my mind started becoming peaceful every day little by little. 'Allah is severe in retribution. Allah is with those who would be patients'. I found consolation on it." Strong farmer said.
"I am sorry." My grandpa said and gave a hug to strong farmer again and my grandpa took the strong farmer with him to Dhaka. And before go to Dhaka, he brought two bulls for the two farmers.

What Kind of Personality does our Grandpa have?

Sometime the behaviors of my grandpa let me to think "what kind of personality does my grandpa has?" "Is he a complicated person or a naïve person?" It was little difficult for me to come to the conclusion about the behaviors of our grandpa. Sometime I think "probably he is just a naïve person in nature but become aggressive just to protect himself from the environment which is always go against the weak people and want to crush them. Probably he is just like a cat who does not want to surrender easily to the dog. And ready for the fierce fight, if it would be needed." People may think why sometime I think he is just a naïve person. In Bangladesh, someone wrote a book about dream. Title: What Did You See At The Dream, And What Could Happen? My grandpa has one such book. When I was just 9/10 years old, he most of the time told me ""can you bring the dream book and cheek "what could happen, if someone see a black cow in the dream"". I just followed his request and read it for him without understand much about it. And I also started believing it like my grandpa. One day Mr. Ansari heard it and started laughing loudly. My grandpa felt little embarrass. And he tried to resist Mr. Ansari. My grandpa argued with Mr. Ansari "dream book is most of the time is right. It gives the correct prediction." Anyway I read the dream book for my grandpa until I did not understood why Mr. Ansari was laughing. One day Mr. Ansari was explaining about the dream. He tried to explain "why do we see the dream?" He said that it is a complicated process of the brain. He continue explained "Most of the time what we think in absent mind that we could see in the dream. For example someone knows person A and he think about that person. And he also knows person B. and he think about that person. He could think a lot of think in his absent mind like mountain, paddy field. Somehow our brain processes all of the thought we think in our absent mind. This thought could be one day old or month/months old. Brain picks something from person A and something from person B and the other though we has in our absent mind. Like Person A was 70 years old use nice cloth I thought. And person B was 50 years old. I may see in the dream that 50 years old man with the same nice dress or like it used by the 70 years old man. Because dream is a very complicated process of the brain which is created by God, sometime God can play with it (if he like). Like some dream could showed by God to some people. Like Prophet Abraham (SAW) saw the dream of sacrificing his son. Prophets were inspired by God. Their thought processes were also inspired by God. So they also could see at their dream what they were thinking. Reading the palm or seeing the dream and tried to interpret it to know what could happen in a person life is created from the desire of the people. They want to stay good and stay out of the trouble. So a person wants to hear the good think. The writer of the dream book just used this technique to fool the people. Sometime they say that bad think also could happen. But in reality reading palm and the dream has nothing to do what could happen in someone life."

Mr. Ansari took a pause and continue "sometime people say that what did I see last night that happened to me today or someone else. But this person absent mildly was thinking of it and that he saw it at the dream and what he was thinking in his absent mind that he actually saw to happen next day. In his absent mind already come to the conclusion what could happen."

Grandpa raise the question about the Prophet Abraham (SAW) and his receiving message from God.

Mr. Ansari said "God has power over everything. He can do whatever he wants. But Koran confirms that no message will come from God for the mankind. He completed the religion of Islam. So we can't expect that God need to give me special instruction to satisfy God when he said to Follow the instruction what was given in Koran and following the prophet are enough to satisfy God. If still some people see in the dream that God is telling him to do something, they should first confirm that that would not go against the Koran and the teaching of our prophet."

My grandpa raise the question about the hadith about the seeing the prophet in the dream.

Mr. Ansari said " I do not know much about it. If it in the hadith, we must have to accept it as a true. At the same time we should know that the hadith is authentic or not. Is this hadith is for us or for the people of his life time."

"do you see the dream of the prophet (SAW)?" Mr. Ansari asked my grandpa.

My grandpa said "no."

Mr. Ansari said "but we see the dream every day at our sleep. What about this dream. This is the dream is the product of the thinking in our absent mind. God says that all the mess we human being are experiencing surrounding us are created by us. Same way our dreams are created by us. What we feed our brain that our brain programs to give us feedback about what are we thinking. Let me give an example. A lot of time I see my hero in the dream is an idiot. It gives me feedback that I do sometime spend to thinking about an idiot. Let me give another example. I saw a dream I am in India for visiting. I am staying in a place which is made of bamboo fence. Big room and a lot of beds. I am the only Muslim on their. Suddenly riot broke out between the Muslim and Hindu. People are being killed. I was scared. All people around me is Hindu. I saw myself in an open space. I fight back. I wake up. My dream is over. Next morning I was thing why did I see that dream? I tried to patch all the information has in the dream and what was in my mind. Riot was broken out the Indian State of Asam and people were killed. I was in Hungary and stay in a Motel and that Motel beds I saw in the dream. I am planning to go to Hungary. I was in the USA to visit my son. I was thinking about September 11 and what happen suddenly to the Muslim. My friend has a house which is made of bamboo and he rent it. And it is always in my mind not to scare because God said to fear him and not to fear his creation. So all of this my thought process and experience somehow my brain programmed for me to show in the dream. Most of the dreams are incomplete. Our brain is very smart. It could modify and could patch one incident to other. So the conclusion is what we feed our brain that we see in the dream to get the feedback what are we thinking about. Good or bad. Smart or dump etc."

Mr. Ansari took a pause and continued "do you think in reality I would myself fight back against hundreds of Hindu people? Answer would be 'no'."

Mr. Ansari took a pause again and said "I would follow the prophet (SAW) and how he escaped from Mecca to Yetrib (Madina). No one knows better than our prophet (SAW) about the existence of God and his power. But our prophets escaped."

"Does Satan has any power to enter our dream?" my grandpa asked.
"absolutely not" Mr Ansari respond.

"God did not give the power to Satan to enter to our dream. God did not give the power to Satan to mess around with us unless we let Satan to mess around with us. God gave us power to control the Satan. Satan can't control us unless we want Satan to control us. Satan promise to God to take the children of Adam (SAW) with him to the hell fire and God gave Satan to do so. But Satan can't do anything unless people would let Satan to play with them. I see a lot of people are helping Satan to fulfill his promise that he would take children of Adam (PBUH) with him to the hell fire and these people often have an angel dress." Mr. Ansari added.

After took a pause Mr. Ansari said to repeat what he tried to say before" Satan has power to capture our thought process. And at the same time God also give us power to repeal the act of Satan by not to let Satan to capture our thought process. This is us who can let Satan to continue play with our thought process. Yes when we let Satan to play with our thought process that we could see at our dream. But the dream I will see tonight, I have no power to control it or to predict it. But I can tell what am I thinking and what am I going to think. Absolutely God did not gave the power to Satan to enter our dream unless we let the Satan to enter our dream though our thought process. Absolutely God did not give the power to control any aspect of our life which we would not able to protect ourselves from Satan. As God said that we the human being are the responsible for all the mess we are experience surrounding on us. And the same way we are responsible for what we see in our dream."

After took a pause Mr. Ansari continue by asking question to grandpa "what does it mean if I would see some one is saying he is the prophet? What do you know about it? Does it mean I will go to the heaven and I am a saint? I never see our prophet and I do not know how he looks like"

Grandpa respond "I don't know."

Mr Ansari said " In this case even I will see someone is saying he is the prophet in my dream, I will keep it secret out of fear that after my death some Muslim would start worshiping me as a saint and will make partnership me with the God. And they will ask for job, marriage to me etc."

"Let me give an example. I went to Azmir, India out of curiosity what is going on there. President of my country went there to visit the place. What I saw on there is totally prohibited in Islam. People on Azmir let people to prostrate to the grave. And people are asking for this dead person for child, job etc. whatever the difficulty they are facing that they are asking to this dead person. Even we Muslim know that after the death of our prophet, he himself has no power to do anything for us. Our prophet does not know what we the followers of him are doing. Azmir becomes a business place for some people. In this situation if I would have authority, I would send my people to stop to worship a human being and let the people to know that what they are doing is prohibited in Islam."

After took a pause Mr Ansari said ""I would restore the God's command. "Worship God and worship him alone.""

It was in my mind what Mr. Ansari told about the dream. But I did not understand it. But after some years, I agree with Mr. Ansari. Mr. Ansari gave the warning to my grandpa about if someone would believe all those things such as palm reader prediction about the future and book like 'what did you see at dream and what could happen'. If someone believe these, God will nullify someone prayer. After my grandpa heard it from Mr. Ansari, he asked the local mosque Imum (leader of the mosque who is kind of pastor) to confirm it. If someone would believe what the palm reader would tell, that person's prayer would not be accepted. Because only God determine peoples destiny and only God knows about the future of a person. After that grandpa destroyed that book which explain about the dream.

What kind of person our grandpa is. This question comes in my mind time to time. Different time the answer come inside of me differently after I hear his different stories. Probably inside of him he is a very kind person to the weak and poor people. But sometime he becomes mad which could even lead him to be in the fighting mood. As a youth, he engaged in fighting easily. He did not control himself much. He did not have that much fear of God at that time because what he know about God at his old age he did not know about it as a young man. Even he knew about God and what God want him to behave, it did not prevent him to violate the command of God. His youthfulness probably prevented him to think much about God and to follow the commands of God. Islam is a way of living according. Muslims have with the commandment of God. His youthfulness overrules the commands of God probably. Be patients. Be kind to the people. Avoid conflict with the people. All these teaching did not appeal to him that much at his young life. As he grows older and the teaching of our prophet (SAW) started appealing in his life, he starting to give up to live with his own desire. When his desire came to overrules God desire, it seemed to me he put a break on his own desire to stop it. Fear of God came in his heart. Even inside of him boil up to engage in fighting with the people to take the revenge, he cooled him down and avoid fighting in old age. At old age he able to transform himself "fears of God to overrule his own desire".

He Is My Mother's Father --☺ Anwar Al-Haqq

What is going on in the society?

At the evening my grandparents, Azim and Jamil came from Noakhali. Next evening, grandma and grandpa were sitting in the living room. Grandpa was reading the newspaper and grandma was weaving a sweater. He was in relax and comfortable mood.
"Mr. Ansari came to invite us this morning for his granddaughter's birthday. He said he don't observe birthday. This is against our religion. This day he became grandpa for first time and he just invite his friends and relatives to share his feeling how happy he was that day. He also invited our grandchildren" grandma told grandpa.
"he told me last week" grandpa said.
"did you buy any gift?"
"off-course I did"
"where is it? What did you buy?" grandma asked.
"it is a secret"
Grandma raised her head and circles her neck with little frustration.
"today is also birthday for one of Jolly's friends. She will take Lilly with her at the birthday's party." grandma said.
"Jolly informed me" grandpa said.
"Jamil and Azim will go with us" grandma said.
"no" grandpa said.
Grandma looked at his face with little angrily.
"when they would be married, would they take me with their wife at the part?" grandpa added.
Grandma's anger went up. Grandpa was sitting comfortably and his eyes were in the newspaper while talking with grandma.
"they will go with their grandma." grandma said angrily.
Grandma took a pause.
"Be preparing to go to Mr. Ansari's house." grandma told grandpa in commanding voice.
Grandma left the living room. Grandpa was sitting comfortable for a while and read the newspaper. It was kind of pleasure for him to raise the anger of my grandma.

After a while Azim and Jamil came out with well dress from their room and walked to come to the living room. They were excited. They were going to the party. Grandma came to the living room. She wearied a Borka, a dress usually a Muslim woman use as a

He Is My Mother's Father --☺ Anwar Al-Haqq

Hijab to cover their head to toe. When my grandma walked at the street, she usually use Borka. Mr. Ansari home was 7 minutes walking distance from my grandpa's home.

Azim, Jamil and grandma were waiting for grandpa at the living room. After a while, grandpa came to the living room with well dress. He had a Sarawani. He was carrying a small box under his right arm.
"grandpa give me the box" Azim said to grandpa.
Grandpa ignored him and pretended that he did not hear anything. They stared walking to go to the Mr. Ansari's house. They were walking in the street. Grandma, Azim, Jamil were walking in front and grandpa was walking behind them. The gift box was under the arm of grandpa.

Mr. Ansari was expecting his guests. So his door was open. It was a small birthday party. Just few friends of Mr. Ansari and close relatives; and his granddaughter's close friend were invited. Mr. Ansari's son lived in the USA. So Mr. Ansari was the only male guardian now in the family. My grandpa arrived to the home of Mr. Ansari. Mr. Ansari received my grandparents, Jamil, Azim with very cordially. He took them to the living room where he met with Mr. Ansari's granddaughter. He gave the gift to the hand of Mr. Ansari's granddaughter. She showed her excitement to get the gift. Grandma went inside to meet the wife of Mr. Ansari, the guests and other household members of Mr. Ansari. Mr. Jalil came before them. His grandson came with him. After a while, Mr. Matin came with his granddaughter. By the time Mr. Matin came to Mr. Ansari home, it was time for the magrib prayer, prayer for the Muslim just after the sun set. They prayed together. After the prayer, all the male adult guests sat down on the sofa in the living room. They were talking.

Mr. Jalil's grandson, and Mr. Ansari's grandson's who is second grade student were playing at the apartment. Azim and Jamil joined with them. Whole apartment become their playing ground. Mr. Ansari's grandson was the center of their attention. He hid and everyone found him out. This time Mr. Ansari's grandson hid behind the sofa where my grandpa was sitting down. Azim and Jamil came to find him out. They were in playing mood. My grandpa tried to get their attention.
"sit quietly next to me" grandpa said to Azim and Jamil.

Azim and Jamil did not pay much attention what my grandpa said. Mr. Ansari gave the hand sign to grandpa to let them to play.
"my whole apartment is the playing ground for my grandson." Mr. Ansari said.
My grandpa got the assurance from Mr. Ansari that they can play. It was hard for my grandpa to tell them not to play in their apartment. But they came to visit Mr. Ansari's home. It was my grandpa's concern.
"in the City of Dhaka, there are not that many playground for the kids" Mr. Matin said.
"yes you are right" Mr. Ansari said.
"when I was in their age and I was living in Commila, my dad 5 acres house was my playground. Now my grandson cornered down in my apartment." Mr. Ansari added.
Everyone nodded their head for approval. Grandpa again got the assurance from Mr. Ansari that it was Ok that Azim and Jamil can play in their apartment. After that, grandpa did not tell them not to play in the Mr. Ansari's apartment. Mr. Ansari was the host. He was little nice to everyone that day than usual.

After a while dinner was served. Grandpa was seemed to be in good mood after the dinner. Good foods were served at the dinner. After ate the dinner, everyone sat comfortably at the living room. Grandpa leaned for a while in the sofa. It looked everyone ate little extra food compare to their regular day. Everyone sat comfortable at the sofa without talking for a while. They gave the food time to settle down in their stomach. Everyone appreciated Mr. Ansari to serve the good food. Mr. Ansari felt little flattered. He showed his modesty. Kids went back to play. They were engage in to show their action to impress each other.
"food was real good" grandpa said.
Mr. Matin, Mr. Jalil and the other people who were present in the living room agreed with my grandpa.
"in Mymansing, does people server the lentil soup before they serve main the course of the food or after the main course of the food?" grandpa asked Mr. Jalil.
"I do not know" Mr. Jalil answer with little suspicious.
It was seemed that he was not expecting to hear this question even he just ate the lentil soup. He did not understand why my grandpa asked that question.
Mr. Matin looked at my grandpa. Mr. Ansari tried to say something

but prevent him not to join in the discussion of 'eating lentil soup'.
"eating lentil soup is important to know when to eat" Mr. Matin said to make Mr. Jalil to feel comfortable.
"you are right" grandpa respond.
"when I came first in Dhaka and lived myself, lentil soup and the rice was the only course for me most of the time. Both were easy to cook. Life was simpler that time like the cooking of the lentil soup" my grandpa added.
Everyone nodded their head to agree with grandpa.
"as the old man said 'as the day is passing, we are embracing the difficulty'. Tomorrow will be the difficult day for us then today." my grandpa said.
Everyone agree with my grandpa.
"I was just married like you and came to Dhaka. I got a job as a bus contractor. Even bus contractor job was only to collect the bus fare, I made enough at least to live honestly. Now a day, bus contractions have to steal money to survive" Mr. Matin said.
Everyone agreed with Mr. Matin.
""I had a degree in Bachelor of Science. I was looking for job. My wife said "why would you work for other? Do business." I agreed with her. I took a course for the Pharmacy technician. After that, her father gave me money to start the Pharmacy business. I was doing well. I never heard of that I have to give someone money every month to run my business or he would send a gang to show me the gun. And that time there were not that many pharmacies. Now Pharmacy is in every corner of the road."" Mr. Matin added.
My grandpa was listening to Mr. Matin with great attention.
"you are right" my grandpa agreed with Mr. Matin.
Grandpa move little to sat even more comfortably.
""My construction business was running well. It was 1972, I had a Government contact for a four storage building. I submitted the paper to get my first payment. I was going to the office to get my payment. Three day I went to the office. I was told that Engineer did not sign the paper. So no payment for me. I came back home. One day, Engineer's assistant took me one corner of the office and told me "look at the brick of this building. They also want to get there share. If one person would eat the whole pie, it would work like the poison. If we all could eat the pie, it would become the food."
Grandpa said "I was trying to understand what does he mean. The assistant eyes were on my face. After a while he started blinking his both eyes same time. His eyes were blinking and looked at my

face.""

Mr. Ansari was also leaning at the sofa. He move forward to say something, but he suppress himself.

Grandpa looked at Mr. Ansari and said "I know what you will tell me. You will tell me that all my nerves are very thick and slow some time. Hard to passed the information through it"

Mr. Ansari shown the satisfaction of the statement of my grandpa without saying anything and smile of his face became wider. He leaned back to sofa again.

Grandpa started "where I was. Oh. The assistant was blinking his both eyes to me. I said oh! My⋯⋯. I heard of it, under the table transaction. But I did not face it so far."

"Assistant told me to be quite. And he told me that the bricks of the wall also have ears. I became quite, but puzzled"

"What percentage would be the share for your bricks? I Asked.

The assistant whispered in my ear. I tried to bargain. He told me that it is a fixed rate. I gave him the money. Next day I saw my check was ready. And I learned from them that the brick of their building office also ask for money and it also has ears. When I beat for the tender, I did not add that money. I felt the money I gave the assist for the engineer was a kind of losing money. My profit went down. Next tender I started to add the money for the engineer. After a few years percentage went up. They were not following their percentage rules. Sometime the percentage they were asking to me, if I gave them, I would just worked for them. But they gave the chance to bargain. One time I got a contact which was close to Dhaka. It was 1986. Some youth threat me if I would not give them the money, they would not let me to work. They said they were the member of a party. They told me that they kept the minister in their pockets . I contact with my brother-in-law Raj. That time he was a SP for the police. He said that there was a politics behind it. If I tell them anything, next day minister would transfer me in the remote area of Bangladesh. So he suggested me to negotiate with them. He called local Police office to make a negotiation with the gang to give me a better deal, to reduce their fee. That's I did. Next tender, I added again for the gang fees. My profit went down. But I continue. Something is better than nothing. Now a day bribe also does not work. Everyone is giving the bribe. You have to compete how much more you would give as a bribe compare to the other people to get their service.""

My grandpa was the person to tell the story and all other to listen the story. My grandpa took a pause and started talking ""My brother-in-law took bribe. His sister-in-law heard it. And said "oh! You took the bribe." She let him the feeling 'taking the bribe was a despicable crime.' Now day bribe is consider as a gift and acceptable in the society. Mother-in-law does not hesitate to cook good food for her son-in-law who accept the bribe and bought gift for them. My grandpa exhaled a big breath.""

My grandpa took a pause and started talking again "My brother-in-law prepare Engineer over doctor for his daughter."

My grandpa became little tired of talking.

"you are right. As we are passing the day, we are giving the Farewell the moral value and inviting immoral value in our society. After a while immoral value is becoming the moral value in the society. No one is standing firmly to prevent it." Mr. Matin said to agree with my grandpa.

Then he stared talking ""about 7/8 years ago, I went to buy chicken. Business man asked me Tk 150 per kilogram. I said that outside Dhaka it is Tk 120 per kilogram. You are asking too much. He said "bring the chicken from outside to here and to stand here to sale chicken, we have to spend at least gang fee TK 20 per kilogram. We have to add it like the VAT. Value Added Tax (VAT) which government impose." I said you are asking TK 10 more for the gang fee. After add the gang fee, it should be TK 140 per kilogram. He gave me a big smile and said "We already invested the money. Money has to bring the money. Giving the gang fee becomes a kind of investment for us." "you are giving this fee. And on return, are you getting anything back from them?" I asked. He said "nothing". "But I am paying all these fees" I told the businessman. "

Mr. Matin took a pause and also exhale a big breath like my grandpa.

It was time to eat the dessert. Mr. Ansari does not like to cut the birthday cake which may go against the religion. But he was not sure about it. So he decided not to buy the birthday cake. Mr. Ansari's wife called Mr. Ansari. She gave the sweet for these old people who already have hard time to move after eat the food. After ate the dessert, my grandpa said good-bye to them and walked to came home with his two grandsons and his wife.

Just can't suppress the temptation sometime

He Is My Mother's Father --☺ Anwar Al-Haqq

Next morning my grandpa was sitting in the living room on his easy chair. He was reading the newspaper. Jolly came to the living room and sat next to grandpa. She bought a magazine with her. She opened a page and started reading it. My grandpas stop reading the newspaper but his eyes were on the newspaper.
"Salma is not coming home for last two weeks. Do you know when she will come? I am expecting her to call me." grandpa said with little sorrow.
Salma is my only sister.
"she is in love" Jolly talked in whispering voice to grandpa.
Grandpa raised his head that he understood the situation when she is not coming home.
"yea! I heard about it. But she did not tell me anything" grandpa said.
"you heard from grandma. It is same to tell grandma and to tell you. Any information she know she must have to tell you. Otherwise her food would not digest." Jolly said little mockingly.
Grandpa looked at her.
"you do not expect her to tell you: I have a boyfriend. Do you?" Jolly added.
"I don't. but I am her grandpa." grandpa said.
Grandpa was trying to say something. But Jolly bought her mouth close to grandpa's right ear. Grandpas stop talking. He moved forward. She was whispering in grandpa's ear. Grandpa was listening her advice. Some time he was showing that he was agreed with her advice. Her advice was making sense to her. He can't ignore her advice. My aunt was coming to the living room. She saw Jolly was whispering to grandpa. After that she did not come to the living room. Jolly was giving the advice to grandpa. After gave the advice and explained to grandpa, Jolly stop. Grandpa put the newspaper on the table. And he leaned backed. He shown that he accepted Jolly's advice. He also has his own plane. So he was thinking.
"a news guest may come. We need to make good food for him" Jolly told grandpa.
"you never know" grandpa said.
Grandpa called the boy who helped us for our household job. He went to the market. And he bought all the good fish, meat and vegetable. And then he went to the sweet shop to buy the sweet.

In the afternoon, Jolly was whispered to Minu. Minu told everyone

that grandpa was sick. He had the breathing problem. Grandpa was in his bed room. Grandma entered the bed room. She was kind of rush to come to the bed room. Grandpa acted that he was sick. When grandma came close to him, he blinked his eye to her. Grandma understood that it was fake. She became annoyed. Her temper went over the roof of the room. Grandpa has asthma which sometime get worse that grandpa has difficult to take the breath. So everyone too it seriously.
"you did again?" grandma said to grandpa with annoying.
Grandpa did not respond to grandma. He blinked his eyes again. It made grandma even more furious.
After a while, Jolly came to grandpa's bed room. She whispered to grandma.
"you two again made a plot" grandma told angrily to Jolly.
Jolly did not respond her. She was calm. She enjoyed to make grandma angry.
Grandpa's cell phone was on the table. Jolly picked it up and called my sister, Salma.
"hello" my sister said.
"hello. I am calling you to give you a bad news." Jolly said.
My sister become worried and asked "what is it?"
"grandpa is sick" Jolly added.
My sister became little panic to hear the message.
"haa" my sister said out of panic.
"grandpa is not very sick. Only he have a breathing problem" Jolly said.
Grandpa twisted his neck to watch the conversation of Jolly. He was enjoying the situation. Grandma even became annoyed.
"are you coming" Jolly asked my sister.
"off-course I am coming" my sister said.
"we will see you soon" Jolly said and hang up the cell phone.
Grandpa enjoyed the whole conversation. He nodded his head to give his approval that Jolly did a good job.

My sister and Nakib, her boyfriend, were sitting in the balcony. And they were drinking tea when Jolly called my sister. Nakib had sandal, pajama and Panjabi, and a woolen cloth as a winter cloth. After my sister hanged up her cell phone, she was rushing to come home.
"let's go" my sister told Nakib.
"me" Nakib respond.

"not you. Is there anyone here?" my sister told Nakib in surprise.
"let's go! Let's Go!!" my sister told Nakib.
She did not even give time to Nakib to change his cloth. They hired a scooter to come home. They were on their way to home.

My parents, my aunts, my uncle, and my aunt's husband were sitting in the balcony and were drinking tea. Minu walked to them.
  She told them seriously "grandpa is sick. He has a breathing problem".
Everyone rushed to come to see grandpa. Minu was watching them. It looked it was kind of fun for her. They found grandma in the corridor. She just came out from their room.
"we heard dad is sick" my uncle asked my grandma.
My grandpa said with rebuff "go see him".
Everyone was looking at each other face. My mother quietly went back to the balcony. Everyone followed my mother. They were drinking the tea which they left behind. My grandma went back to the bed room. She was observing the situation. She looked still mad. Grandpa blinked his eye to her which made her even more mad.

After a while my mother broke the silence.
"dad pretended that he was sick" my mother said with uncertainty.
"who gave him advice this time Jolly or Montu" my uncle said.
"who could give such advice to dad? I saw in the morning Jolly was whisper in dad ears" my aunt said.
Everyone showed that they understood what was going on. They were drinking tea quietly.

Jolly went out of the bed room of grandpa and went to my brother's room. She knocked the room of my brother. My brother came out. She was talking with my brother that they discussing something serious. After a while my brother went to his room and Jolly went to the living room. Few minute later, my brother came out from his room. A Stethoscope, paper napkin, and alcohol pad were in his hand. He walked to grandpa's bed room. Jolly went to the living room.

Azim and Jamil were walking in in front of grandpa's store. The store keeper came out from the store and tried to get Azim and Jamil's attention.
"Azim" store keeper called loudly.

He Is My Mother's Father -- ☺   Anwar Al-Haqq

Store keeper seemed worried.
Azim and Jamil stood up and walked to him.
"what happened?" Jamil asked.
"your grandpa is sick" store keeper told.
They rushed to see my grandpa. On the way to my grandpa's bed room, they met with grandma at the corridor..
"grandma! Grandma!! We heard grandpa is sick" Azim told and showed his concern.
"Go see your grandpa" grandpa told in rude way.
Jamil looked at Azim.
"he did it again" Azim said.
Azim walked at the corridor to go to the grandpa's bed room. He was in mood like someone annoyed him and he was going to beat him. Jamil followed him. Grandma walked to the living room. At the door of my grandpa, Azim and Jamil stood up for a while. And become normal. Jamil knocked the door.
"can we come to see you?" Jamil asked.
"yes! You can" grandpa responded.
 He acted like he was sick and he had hard time to talk.
Grandpa gave the sign to my brother to pretend that he was examining him. Jamil and Azim walked nicely inside my grandpa's bed room. They showed that nothing happened.
"can I examine you?" my brother asked my grandpa.
"sure" grandpa said and took off his shirt.
Grandpa was complying with my bother while he was examining him. Azim and Jamil sat next to grandpa. My brother put his stethoscope in my grandpa's chest.
"can you breath in and out for me" my brother asked.
Grandpa did it but acted that it was hard for him to do.
"lung looked clear to me" my brother said.
"nothing happened to him" Azim said.
"are you a doctor? Are you?" grandpa said little loudly to Azim.
He acted out to that he was mad what Azim said.
"get out from here. Sit on there" grandpa said and showed them where to sit.
"are you two a doctor? What do you know about disease?" grandpa added.
Azim and Jamil moved to sit even close to grandpa.
"at least we know that if someone become sick they don't talk loudly" Jamil respond.
"hay! You two! If you don't know anything don't talked about it" my

brother said to Azim and Jamil and turned his face away from them to the door.
He was going to laugh but suppress it. My sister-in-law out of curiosity want to see what was going on. The door of my grandpa's bed room was open. She was going to give a look through the door. My brother saw her.
"Shawn" my brother tried to get attention of my sister-in law. She stood up at the door.
"would you please come to examine our grandpa" my brother asked my sister-in-law.
My grandpa because little uneasy. My sister-in-law walked to the room. But she was not enthusiastic to examine grandpa in that circumstance. My brother cleaned the ear piece of the stethoscope with the paper napkin and with the alcohol pad. And he gave to my sister-in-law to examine my grandpa. My grandpa looked at my brother. My brother saw it, but he turned his face to the other side. Pretend that he did not understand the feeling of grandpa. My sister-in-law went to examine my grandpa against her will.
"how long do you have breathing problem?" my sister-in-law asked my grandpa nicely.
Azim and Jamil were going to give a big laugh to hear this question. But they showed that they suppress that feeling by putting their hands on their mouth. My grandpa looked at them with annoyed. My sister-in-law did not wait for the answer of our grandpa. My sister-in-law warmed the stethoscope by rubbing it.
"I will put my stethoscope on your chest to listen your lung, is that be ok with you?" my sister-in-law asked my grandpa.
My grandpa nodded his head for the approval. My sister-in-law put the stethoscope on the chest of my grandpa.
"can you breath in and out?" my sister-in-law asked my grandpa.
Grandpa was following her instruction. Jamil and Azim were smiling and at the same time they put their hands over their mouth to suppress their laugh. Grandpa gave them quick looked with annoyed. But he did not tell them anything.
"can you take a deep breath? And breath in and out." my sister-in-law added.
My grandpa took a deep breath and out the breath.
"lung is clear to me" my sister-in-law said.
Azim and Jamil tried to laugh, but they showed that they were suppressing it.
"all is hoax. I told before. Nothing happened to him." Azim said.

Grandpa again gave a quick look to him with annoyed.
"there are a lot of dust in the street. When someone walked in the dust, sometime it could give the difficulty in breathing." my sister-in-law said.
My grandpa nodded his head.
"why some people eat their own food at their own house and would drive out the buffalo from the forest? I don't understand it. What benefit has in it?." Jamil said.
"just see a construction site and stood up to count the brick. I don't understand it. What benefit has in it?" Azim said with shaking his head right side to left.
Grandpa again looked at them with annoying.
"Hay! You Two. Did I not told you two not to talk about a subject which you don't understand?. What our grandpa understand that you two understand not." my brother looked at them and said to them with smiling. It was seemed to my what my brother told to them before that they were repeating to grandpa.
My grandpa looked at my brother. Grandpa was agreed with my brother.
"let's go" Azim told Jamil.
 Both Azim and Jamil stood up and left.
"I have to go" My sister-in-law said and followed them.

My mother some time came out from the balcony to see what was going on without asking any one question to anyone. She just walked through the corridor and go back to the balcony again.

My sister's scoter stop at the gate. She rushed to see my grandpa.
"what happened to my grandpa" my sister said little loudly at the corridor with concern.
Everyone heard her. But no one was at the corridor at that time.
"she is here" my grandpa said and looked at my brother.
My brother signal my grandpa to act like a sick person. And he became like a sick person.
My mother came out from the balcony after she heard my sister voice. Before my mother reach to the corridor which take from the gate to my grandpa's bed room, my sister already entered the room. Grandma stood up from the chair at the living room. Jolly hold her hand. My mother went back to the balcony.
"wait for a while" Jolly told grandma.
"let her to go first to see grandpa" Jolly added.

After a while they came out from the living room and standing at the corridor.
"let me check what is going on in grandpa's bed room." Jolly told grandma.
Jolly walked to the bed room of grandpa and give a quick look and came back to grandma.
"the boy is not with her" Jolly told grandma.
"you think that Salma would just tell the boy and the boy would rush to come here" grandma said mockingly.
Jolly became worried.
From the corridor, she walked to the stair. Grandma followed her. From the stair, they could see the street. They saw a man was standing in front of the gate. It was looked that he was in trouble.
"I think that's him" Jolly said and shown her excitement. What she was looking for that she found.
"can you see the future groom of Salma" Jolly said to grandma.
Grandma little rushed to see him.
"where?" grandma asked.
"do you not see a man is standing at the gate?" Jolly said.
My grandma looked at that young man with very care.
"did you see how my grandpa made him an idiot. Love made him an idiot. What a love? He is waiting at the gate without being shame." Jolly said.
"don't said him an idiot. He is just a naïve person." my grandma said.
"you already fall in love to him. If grandpa would see him at this situation, he would say that who gave him the security job and he would add that he does not have any quality be a security guard. He can't even stand firmly." Jolly said.
"looked at him. He is falling apart." Jolly added.
Grandma was listening Jolly with smile but showed that she was not totally agree with her.
Shop keeper saw my sister came with a man. She went inside but the man was waiting and standing at the gate. He was in puzzle for a while. Then he came out from the store. Without saying anything to the man, he walked through the gate and met Jolly and grandma at the stair.
"Salma aunty came with a man. He is standing at the gate. Do you want me to bring him to the living room?" the store keeper said to Jolly and my grandma.
My mother was walking at the corridor at that time. She stop when

He Is My Mother's Father --☺ Anwar Al-Haqq

she heard the voice of the store keeper. And she walked to close to grandma and Jolly. Jolly and grandma did not realize that my mother was walking toward them. Their attention was to see the man how he was standing at the gate.
"he is not qualified yet to walk through the gate of this home and then walked through the stair and from there to the corridor to walked to go to the living room and to sit at the living room" Jolly said little rudely and also showing the way from the gate to the living room .
My grandma nodded for the approval.
"let him to sit at the shop" Jolly added.
My grandma was showed that she was fully agreed with Jolly. My mother was watching them from the back and was listening their conversation. But Jolly and grandma did not see her.
"give him a bottle of Pepsi" Jolly said.
"Ok" shop keepers said and turn back and walked to come to the store.
"give him a newspaper too" Jolly added.
Jolly and grandma turned their face back to come to the corridor. They saw my mother. Jolly became little polite to see my mother. But she did not say anything. My mother also turned back to come to the balcony without saying anything.
"hum! He is a doctor. But still not qualify. What are they looking for their granddaughter and cousin?" my mother said herself with smile while she was walking at the corridor.
From the corridor, she went to the balcony.
"Salam came?" my mother tried to get my father attention.
"when did she come?" my father pretend that he did not hear her voice.
"A little while ago, there is a new guest with her." mother said.
"who is the new guest?" my uncle asked out of curiosity.
"You will see" my mother said.
My uncle suppressed his curiosity. My father stood up. He went to his bed room. After a while, he went out from the house without telling anyone anything.

After entered at the bed room of the grandpa, my sister saw my grandpa was sick and my brother was taking care of him.
"what happened to grandpa?" my sister asked worriedly.
"he have difficult to breath. And some time also difficult to talk. But nothing is life threatening" my brother responded and gave the

assurance of my sister.
Grandpa showed that he had a problem in breathing. My brother cleaned the stethoscope with the alcohol pad and with the napkin, and gave to my sister.
"go and check the lung of our grandpa" my brother told my sister.
She went to examine grandpa. Jolly entered the room. She was watching how my sister was examining the lung of our grandpa. Grandpa showed that he was very eager to be examine. He was complying with my sister. After finished the examination, she stood up. She looked worried. She wanted to re-examine the lung of the grandpa.
"what did you find?" my brother asked my sister.
"lung is cleared to me." my sister said worriedly.
"let check the lung again. Did I miss anything?" she talked herself.
"that's OK. He is fine. You do not need to examine him again. Just come here." my brother said.
Grandpa showed that he was eager to let my sister to reexamine him again.
My sister followed by brother's instruction. She went close to my brother. Jolly went close to grandpa.
"grandpa walked through the sand. As you know that he is a stubborn person. He is the person don't want to listen anyone. That is the cause."
Grandpa moved a little from his position after he hear that my brother told him stubborn.
"if he had a breathing problem, I could hear the whizzing." my sister said,
"that right" my brother respond.
My brother was explaining all the medical subjects. My sister had half attention to my brother. She felt uneasy. It was like she was missing something and she was looking for it. Grandpa was watching her activity. Jolly went close to grandpa.
"he came too." Jolly told grandpa in whispering voice.
Grandpa showed that he was enjoying the situation. He signed Jolly to stand in front of him that he could hide him to watch my sister. Jolly stood in front of him.
"how do you feel grandpa?" Jolly asked.
"Little better" grandpa responded.
"any breathing problem?"
"Little. I am getting better." grandpa said.
"you are speaking better too. It is almost clear" Jolly said.

He Is My Mother's Father --☺ Anwar Al-Haqq

Grandpa was watching my sister and nodded his head for approval. "go and bring the boy" grandpa said to Jolly in whispering voice.

Jolly went to the store to bring Nakib, the boyfriend of my sister. Nakib was reading a newspaper. His face was behind the newspaper. A Pepsi bottle was on the table. He did not even take a sip from it. Jolly walked close to Nakib. Nakib understood that someone was coming toward him. He put downed the newspaper.
"Hello" Jolly said with smiling.
"Hello" Nakib said also with smiling.
"Is your name Mr. Nakib? Did you come with Salma?" Jolly asked with smile.
"yes. My name is Nakib." Nakib respond and stood up and put the newspaper on the table.
"My named is Jolly. I am the cousin of Salma." Jolly said.
"nice to meet with you" Nakib said.
"Nice to meet you too. What a strange! Why are you sitting at the store? Come with me." Jolly said to Nakib.
The shop keeper was trying to say something, but he suppressed himself. Nakim was getting shy. They stared walking. Jolly saw that Nakib did not take the Pepsi bottle. She walked two steps back to take the Pepsi bottle.
"you would not have time to read the Newspaper." Jolly said to Nakib.
Nakib was listening but he was not responding.
"all I hear from Salma for last six month only Nakib! And Nakib!! And Nakib!!! Some time I just put my fingers in my ears. When she did not like that, I put cotton pad before I could meet with her" Jolly was talking while walking with Nakim.
Nakib was just listening. Jolly was at the door of grandpa's room. She knocked the door.
"grandpa! Can I come in?" Jolly said.
"yes you can" grandpa said in faint voice.
My sister looked at grandpa. Suddenly he became sicker. She looked and became annoyed. Jolly and Nakib entered the room. Jolly introduce Nakib to my brother. Grandpa was watching the situation. My sister was getting little anger some time. And after that she was getting back to normal again. My brother clean the ears piece of the stethoscope with the alcohol pad then cleans it with the napkin and gave it to Nakib.
"grandpa have problem in breathing. You came to see him. You are

a doctor. If you want you can examine his lung" my brother said to Nakib.

My sister temper went up. After that it became normal again. My grandpa was watching the situation. Jolly went close to my sister. "Pepsi bottle. Pepsi for Nakib Bhai." Jolly told my sister and gave it to my sister. She kept holding the Pepsi bottle. But she did not feel comfortable to keep hold the Pepsi bottle of Nakib. Nakib's Pepsi bottle made her uneasy. Grandpa was enjoying the situation. But he was suppressing his feeling. My brother requested Nakib to examine my grandpa. To keep my brother request, Nakib went to examine grandpa.

"grandpa are you ready? Can Nakib examine your lung?" my brother asked my grandpa.

"sure" my grandpa said.

Grandpa was very interested to be examined. He forgot that he was a patient; and he had a problem in breathing and problem in talking. Nakib put the stethoscope on his chest. My brother saw that my sister was not comfortable to keep holding the Pepsi bottle.

"doc! Do you know how the heart sound like?" my grandpa asked Nakib.

My brother smile to hear what grandpa asked Nakib, but tried to suppress him smile.

"Nakib! Grandpa probably wants you to listen his heart sound. Would you please listen his heart sound?" my brother told Nakib. Nakib listen the lung and also the heart sound.

"heart has regular rate and rhythm. No murmur. Lung is clean on auscultation. No whizzing and rhonchi. Nakib told my brother.

"good" my brother said.

My sister was still keep holding the Pepsi Bottle. Still she was uncomfortable to keep holding the Pepsi bottle.

"give the Pepsi bottle" my brother said to my sister and put it on the table.

My sister went out of the room. Jolly went to stand in front of grandpa. While my brother was talking with Nakib, Jolly pretend that she went to talk with my grandpa.

"how do you feel grandpa? Jolly asked grandpa.

"little better" grandpa respond.

Grandpa was looking at Nakib. But he was pretending that he was talking with Jolly.

"grandpa looked at his feet. Salma dragged him to bring here. She did not even give him time to change his cloth." Jolly said in

whispering voice. Grandpa seemed happy. Nakib heard they were talking but pretend that he was not giving any attention to it.
"grandpa you have a breathing problem" Jolly said.
"Oh" grandpa said and he pretend that he was sick.
My brother was explaining to Nakib what happened to grandpa.
"our grandpa is a stubborn type person. He does not listen to anyone. Even he does not want to listen to our grandma. We told him not to walk at the dust. But he told us that all his establishments were originated from the dust. Now dust is irritating the airway of his lung. And he had breathing problem. I gave him inhaler and he is getting better." my brother explained to Nakib.
My grandpa moved from his place to hear the word stubborn. But he did not say anything. Jolly walked out of the room. She went to the living room. My sister and grandma were in the living room. My grandma was smiling and my sister looked angry. My grandma was trying to cool her down. My sister became furious to see Jolly.
"you! You are the one who gave this advice to grandpa" my sister told angrily.
"what I did. Grandma better you judge between us. What I did" Jolly said very softly and pretend that she was a naïve person.
My sister angry went up then come down. My grandma tried to cool her down.
"his situation would be like the story of cowboy and the tiger. One day in the jungle, a cowboy was walking, suddenly he was screaming Tiger! Tiger!! Everyone came to rescue him. But when people came close to him, he was laughing. He did it two times. One day tiger really came to attack him. He was screaming Tiger! Tiger!! This time no one came to rescue him. And tiger ate him." My sister told the story.
Jolly and grandpa were listening with great attention. They did not interrupt her. Her anger was getting down.
"we have just one grandpa. If we do not take care him. Who will take care him." Jolly said slowly and somberly.
My grandma nodded her head for approval. That made my sister even more mad. My sister touched the chin of my grandma with affection, but also with little rude.
"old lady! Know very well how to support someone." my sister said.
My grandma stood up and said angrily "you bought a boy. You did not even feel responsible to tell us that you are going to bring a new guest at our home. Let see what Minu is cooking for the dinner."
My sister was looking with annoying to my grandma. Jolly looked at

He Is My Mother's Father --☺   Anwar Al-Haqq

my sister.
Jolly said   somberly " grandma also have right to be counter anger if she want".
"You! You are behind of all these plot." my sister told Jolly with rebuff.
"supporting each other" my sister added mockingly.
"what I did?" Jolly said.
"You are pretending that you are the angel. An innocent." my sister said mockingly.
My grandma left the room.
On the way she was talking herself "I am her grandma. This is her duty to support me. And to follow what I have been said. No more support to anyone. Everyone have to support me. I have to command everyone. No one have to command me. I am their grandma.".

My dad went to the market. He bought a big fish and fruits. Minu was on the corridor. My mother was coming from the balcony to the corridor. My father just entered from the stair to the corridor.
Minu tried to get my mother attention and said with little loudly "did you see the act of uncle? Grandpa already filled the refrigerator with fish, meat and vegetable. He bought sweet, fruit this morning too."
My mother looked at my father. My father looked little embarrasses. After that my mother looked at Minu "that's OK. You do not have to worry to put the fish in the refrigerator. I will cook the fish for the dinner."
After that my mother looked at my father "you did a good job. Dad forgot to buy a buffalo fish. You daughter liked the fried buffalo fish".
My mother took the fish from my father. And Minu took the fruit's bag and went to the kitchen. My dad walked to the balcony.

At night we sat for dinner. Only eight people could sit at the dinner table. My grandpa sat to eat dinner with Jolly, Azam, my brother, my sister, Nakib, and me. Jolly and my brother sat next to my grandpa on two opposite side of the table. Nakib sat between me and my brother. Azam sat next to Jolly. My sister sat just opposite of my grandpa. I felt our table could be big enough that Jamil, Azim and Lilly also could sit with us. But the table was only for 8 people. We request our grandma to sit with us. But she became shy. My sister was still little mad. My grandpa was in good mood. He enjoyed making my sister mad. Grandpa was not paying much attention that my sister was mad.

"surrounded by all the advises." my sister said mockingly to grandpa.

Grandpa did not pay attention. He was smiling. My brother was giving the food at the plate of Nakib. He was saying not to give him any more. My grandpa told a story that How he made a bet with his friend and ate half kilogram of Basmati rice, one fish which was half kilogram weight. He also ate two legs of the roasted chicken and a small cup of beef curry.

In the middle of the story of my grandpa, Jolly made an interruption.

"can I gave little rice or a piece of fish or beef or chicken" Jolly asked grandpa.

"I am full" grandpa said.

Grandpa was more interested to talk then to eat.

"Can't eat like before" grandpa added.

"just a piece of a meat and a small piece of fish" Jolly requested grandpa.

She gave a piece of meat and fish in grandpa's plate.

"grandpa! tell the story: usually first day of Eid-ul- fiter, your father used to sacrifice one cow. He thought there could be shortage of meat. Next day he sacrificed a goat." Jolly told while she was taking food at her own plate and also giving food at her brother's plate.

My grandpa looked at Jolly with smile. Grandpa looked at her for a while. Then he started telling his story what technique he used to win the bet. I was going to tell my grandpa that if anyone would eat that much food, he or she could automatically have problem to expend the lung. Stomach would prevent to expand the lung. And automatically any person could have breathing problem. But I suppress myself not to tell anything that day for the sake of the new guest. I ate the food quietly.

After ate the food, my sister wanted to go back to her apartment. She have to be at the hospital floor 6 o'clock in the morning. She gave a big hug to my grandparents. But still she was mad to my grandpa. My grandpa was enjoying the whole situation. He told the driver to give them the ride to go to their apartment. They also said good-bye to my parents and to my brothers, his wife, all my uncles, aunts, and my cousins. My niece was sleeping.

"your daughter. Trained by her dad. Also got her dad temper. If become mad, it stay whole day. I told you all my life not to indulge the daughter. But you did not listen to me. Mad to grandpa, grandma, Jolly. everyone" my mother said to my dad while she was walking to their room with my dad.

My dad was listening and was smiling while walking with my mother. It was seemed that he was a happy man.

Help the parents what they need on their journey

Next evening grandma was sitting at the balcony. Grandpa came from the mosque and sat close to grandma at the balcony. He was looking at the newspaper. My grandma was weaving a sweater. After a while Jolly came and sat close to grandma. Five minutes later my uncle came with his cell phone. He also bought a card to insert into the cell phone.
"mom will go tomorrow morning to her father's house. Insert the card into the cell phone and gave it to mom" my uncle told Jolly and left.
"Ok" Jolly said.
Jolly took the cell phone from my uncle and insert the card inside the cell phone. Then she pressed some number. My grandpa cell phone started ringing. My grandpa's cell phone was in his Panjabi's pocket. He spring up in his chair and pick the cell phone from his Panjabi's pocket. He saw the number was displayed at his cell phone was his son's cell phone number. He gave a looked at Jolly.
"What I did? I am just testing her cell phone." Jolly pointed to grandma.
Grandpa showed that he understood what the purpose was for Jolly to call in his cell phone.
He just said "O".
Grandpa put his cell phone to his ear.
"grandpa do you hear me?" Jolly asked grandpa.
Grandpa nodded his head that he was listening to Jolly. Grandma was just observing the situation without telling anything. Next morning her brother came to pick her up to take to their house

which is in Noakhali.

Grandpa became little kind to Azim in the absence of Grandma

Two days later after grandma went to Noakhali, grandpa was sitting on his easy chair at the living room. He was reading the newspaper. After a while, Azim came to the living room. Grandpa lowered his newspaper to give a looked at him. Azim looked little unhappy. Little regretting. Grandpa did not say anything to him. Azim took a Magazine. He pretended that he was reading it. But he was also showing mental uneasiness. He open the magazine. Then close to leave it on the table. Grandpa lowered his newspaper and was observing the situation. He was trying to understand what happened to Azim.
"grandpa" Azim said.
"yes" grandpa respond with affection.
"grandma went to Noakhali. If I would go with her, what could be the problem? Yesterday they had a tug-of-war. Her team won." Azim said with little somberly.
Grandpa looked at Azim and said with little surprise "your grandma also called you to tell these. I and Jolly were already informed about her victory."
"grandma told also these to Jamil" Azim said.
"she told also to Jamil!" grandpa said in little surprise.
 "Anyway, the question you asked, I am also asking the same question last 48 years: what would be wrong, if I would go with her? But it is their root meeting. We need to be respectful to their root." grandpa added.
"I am also grandma's root" Azim said.
Grandpa looked at Azim with affection and said "her family members do not consider you as their root. They want the pure root."
And he tried to remember what Azim and Jamil did in Noakhali when they went with them. They were jumping from the tree to the pond. Cow was dragging him on the courtyard. After that he tried imagine what could happened if Azim and Jamil were with their grandma. They were with their grandma's team and helped her to win in the tug-of-war. They were pulling hard as hard as they could.

After sitting quietly at the chair for a while, grandpa told Azim "you

He Is My Mother's Father -- ☺   Anwar Al-Haqq

grandma did not take us with her and played tug-of-war. We will go to the zoo. Tell Jamil, Rontu to be ready at 1 o'clock. After eat lunch, we will go to the zoo. Now is 9 o'clock. You have 4 hours to prepare to go to the zoo."
I was not at home in the morning. A flush of light came out from Azim's face. He went out of the room with joy. He told Jamil to be ready at 1 o'clock. Then they were looking at me. But they did not find me.

After they ate lunch, driver bought the car at out gate. I came home from my friend's house. I was listening the Rap Music.
Yu! Yu!!
Story of my niece! Story of my niece!! Story of my niece!!!
She grabbed my nose
She grabbed my nose.
I said "Oooooohhhhhh!
She laughed! She laughed Hahahahahaw!!

Yu! Yu!!
Story of my niece! Story of my niece!! Story of my niece!!!
She grabbed my nose
She grabbed my nose.
I said "Hahahahaw"
She laughed! She laughed hahahahaw!!

Yu! Yu!!
Story of my niece! Story of my niece.
She grabbed my nose
She grabbed my nose
I said "oh-ha! Oh-ha!Oh-ha!!! And cried.
She laughed! She laughed ha-ha-ha-ha-haw.

Azim and Jamil came close to my door. They knocked my door. I opened the door. They wanted to talk with me. And I turned off the cassette player.
"Rontu Bhaya, grandpa want you to go with us at the zoo." Jamil told me with big smile and excitement.
"me" I respond with surprise.
"I have a meeting with my friend in the evening" I added.
"Rontu Bhaye" Azim said with surprise.
"grandpa said that we would have horse ride, elephant would give

us a circle" Jamil told me with joy.
I saw the excitement of Azim and Jamil. If grandpa, my mother know that they were disappoint by me that could also hurt them. Against my own will, I joined with them to go to the zoo. So I tried to get the share of their joy. I showed them that there was no excitement has in this world except to go to the zoo and have a horse ride; and sitting on top of the elephant and elephant to walked to make a circle. They were excited to get me with them. Grandpa came out from his room. He also looked happy. He also liked to go to the zoo.

Grandpa sat at the front seat. I was in the middle of the back seat of the car. Azim and Jamil were right and left side of me respectably. Driver started the car. Destination of the car was the Dhaka Zoo. About 1.30 we came to the Zoo. Grandpa went out of the car. He looked a very happy person. Jamil and Azim were following him very obediently. We went inside the Zoo. We first visited the different cage of the animals. After that we went to get the horse ridge. There was only one horse that day. So, only one person could get the ride. I, Jamil and Azim got the horse ridge. Grandpa was watching us with great attention. It was spectacular for my grandpa to watch that Azim and Jamil were getting the horse ride. Then we went to the elephant cage. I, Jamil and Azim got a ride from the elephant same time. Azim and Jamil looked very happy as was our grandpa. After we got the elephant ride, we were walking inside the zoo. Grandpa took his cell phone out of his Panjabi pocket. He pressed some number. Then he gave it to Jamil.
"talk with your grandma. Tell her that you had a horse ride and elephant also gave you a ride." grandpa told Jamil.
Jamil said "hello grandma"
While Jamil was talking with grandma, grandpa said little seriously "she can have a tug-and-war. You can have a horse ride. Tell her." I saw my grandpa was taking the revenge.
"I have a horse ride, grandma" Jamil said with joy.
"you did good job" grandma respond. But she did not take it seriously. It was out of expectation for Jamil and grandpa.
"explain to her what is horse ride" grandpa told Jamil.
Grandma was in mood to give the advice then to listen about the horse ride. We the grandkids of her were always the subject to get her advice. She is the advice bombardier compare to our Grandpa. I hardly saw our grandpa to give advice to any of his grandchildren except a few occasions. One of this occasion was just after the

marriage of my brother. My brother took the shower at noon and came to the living room. He sat next to grandpa and took few pages of the newspaper and started reading it. Grandpa raised his head from reading the newspaper and asked my brother "how do you feel today?"
"not bad" my brother respond.
"frequent taking shower is not good for health. In the winter season, it could let you to have a cold" grandpa told softly to my brother and started reading the newspaper with deep concentration. Grandpa's advice made my brother thoughtful and at the same time bewildering. He thought for a while and gave concentration to reading the newspaper again.

Anyway, probably grandpa think that grandma is enough to give us advice. Her advices are enough for us. Jamil was trying to tell her know about the Horse ride. But her advice faded away Jamil's afford to tell her about the horse ride. Jamil's excitement to tell her about the horse ride faded away by getting the advice from the grandma. So was the grandpa's plan.
"grandma…" Jamil tried to say something to grandma.
"listen. Road is not safe at night. Did you bring your warm cloth with you?" grandma asked.
"Yes! grandma" Jamil respond.
"did your grandpa, Azim and Rontu brought the warm cloth with them?" Grandma asked.
"yes! grandma" Jamil respond without showing excitement to tell the story of the horse ride rather he tried to nicely answer the questions of the grandma.
Grandpa's face was getting stony. Everything was not going on about his plan.
"this cold is totally bad. Don't stay long time outside" grandma said.
"OK grandma" Jamil respond with dried face.
"is Rontu close to you?" grandma asked Jamil.
"he is standing next to me" Jamil respond.
"give the cell phone to him" grandma told Jamil.
"OK grandma" Jamil said and gave the cell phone to me.
"grandma" I said
"listen. Street is not safe at night. Before sun set, go back to home. Don't stay long time in the cold weather. Dust is everywhere" grandma started give me advice.
I was grimacing my face over the cell phone to express that she

was giving me too much advice. My grandpa looked at me with annoying. He did not like that I was giving a grimace my face to grandma. But he did not tell me anything. After gave me 15 minute advice, my grandma said to me that her cousins were waiting for her. After 2 hours she would called at home. And she hanged up the cell phone.

I came close to grandpa and told him "grandma ordered you to go home before sun set".

Grandpa did not like the word 'Order'. He looked at me again with annoying which was my favorite thing to do to bring out of him. After walked 15 minutes at the Zoo, he started walking toward the exit gate of the zoo. He was not telling us anything. We were following him. Driver was waiting for us at the gate. Grandpa walked to the car to sit at the front sit. We got on the car to come home.

After 2 days, my grandpa was reciting the Quran at his room. His younger daughter came in his room to make the bed, swept the room, organized the room and the closet for her father. After she made the room perfect for her dad, my aunt left the room. After a while, Jolly knocked my grandpa's door. Grandpa was reciting the Koran.

"can I come in grandpa" Jolly asked grandpa.

Grandpa took time to finish the sentence of the Koran. Jolly was waiting for a while at the door.

"sure" grandpa respond with affection.

Jolly came inside the room. She did not look at grandpa and did not say a word to grandpa. Grandpa was reciting the Koran. Jolly straight went to the bed. Grandpa was observing her out of curiosity. She walked to be close to grandpa's bed. Suddenly with one forceful pull, she took off the bed cover from the bed. Grandpa jumped up and shown little panic. Jolly fold the bed cover liked she was making a soccer ball. Then she shake it couple of time. After that she spread put the bed cover on top of the bed. Grandpa was observing her activity and was pretending that he was reading the Koran. After made the bed cover a soccer ball, she took one of the pillow. And suddenly with little forcefully and in one pull, she took the pillow case out of the pillow. Grandpa jumped even more higher than before and became even more panic. She folded the pillow case like the soccer ball and left the pillow case next to the pillow. Jolly was talking herself "she had a tug-of-war. Picnic. Catching fish. Lot of fun. Root meeting. Nothing but fun".

Grandpa understood her plot. Smile replaced the panic in his face behind the Koran. He was trying to understand her plot. Jolly took another pillow and did the same. She did the opposite what my aunt did. She disorganized the room, closet. After disorganized the room, she left the room without saying a word to grandpa. After Jolly left the room, grandpa finished the recitation of the Koran. He pulled out two of his dirty shirt from the closet and threw it at the floor. He disorganized the chairs of the room. After that, grandpa came out of the room, and met Jolly at the balcony. Grandpa went close to her.
"how are you doing grandpa?" Jolly asked grandpa.
"I am fine" grandpa responded with smile but pretend that nothing happened.
Jolly bring her face close to grandpa's right ear and was whispering. Grandpa's face was telling that he was getting very good advice from Jolly and very important. It was very serious. He was listening with good attention. He was not disagreeing with Jolly. After a while, Jolly talked little loudly.
"you will sit down at your room. You will sit down with a calculator, rent collection book, utility book, tax book. You will show that at your room you are busy to do with all of your account." Jolly told grandpa.
Grandpa looked at up and think for a while. It looked like he took the advice of Jolly seriously.

  Few minutes later, grandma's brother Deputy Police Commissioner gave my grandma the ride to bring her home. It was 9 o'clock in the morning. Her brother was in his Police Uniform. He came out from his car and opened the door for my grandma out of respect to his older sister. In Bangladesh people thinks older sister should be respected the way they respect their mother. Police Commissioner Raja never forgot it. My grandma came out of the car. From the balcony, we could see the street. When grandpa saw grandma and her brother, he came out from the balcony to the street to greet this brother-in-law. Jolly was monitoring the situation from the balcony. My brother was walking toward Jolly. Grandpa and his brother-in-law were talking very dearly. Grandpa gave a quick looked to grandma. So did grandma. Grandpa was talking with her brother. Jamil and Azim saw that grandma came with her brother. They run to greet her. Grandma gave them the hug. They missed their grandma.

He Is My Mother's Father -- ☺ Anwar Al-Haqq

"Iqbal can you open the trunk of the car?" grandma asked the driver.
Driver open the trunk of the car. Azim and Jamil helped grandma to take her suitcase out from the car and take to her room. She also bought some coconut and betel-nut from Noakhali which were in the jute bags. There was two jute bags and her suitcase. Azim and Jamil were carrying one bag at a time. So they had three trip to take the three bags. Grandma was supervising Azim and Jamil.
My brother stood next to Jolly. Jolly was watching grandpa that he was talking with her brother-in-law.
"Nice chat is going on for sure." my brother said by pointing to my grandpa and his brother-in-law.
"still he do not know who our grandpa is. He tie the hands and hang it to the roof" Jolly told while she was watching grandpa and his brother-in-law.
"he just held the hands of his brother-in-law and monitor the situation from the next room. Sweet was offered." my brother said while he also was watching my grandpa and his brother-in-law.
"can you asked him, did grandpa really hold him at his father's office?" Jolly said to my brother.
"one day we will cook good food and we will invite this Police office. Then we will ask him about this incidence to get the truth. Today it seemed to me he does not have time. He will go to the office from here." my brother told to Jolly.
"I have to go. It is my duty to give her a welcome to home" Jolly left the balcony and walked to give the welcome to grandma.
"good morning grandma! How do you feel?" Jolly asked grandma.
My grandpa some time gave a look to see what Jolly was doing with the grandma.
 "you don't have to talk with me" grandma respond.
She looked dissatisfy to Jolly.
"what I did?" Jolly said with little sobering voice.
She showed that she was the innocent person. But did not understand why her grandma was dissatisfied to her. Jolly went to give my grandma a hug.
"you don't have to give me a hug" grandma said to Jolly.
"every time I called and asked where is our honorable lady. Honorable lady is at her friend's house" Grandma added with mockingly.
"Haa!" Jolly said and looked at grandma. She moved her head a little away from grandma. Her hands were on grandma's shoulders. She

felt that grandma said her 'an honorable lady' to insult her and she became insulted. She was shocked. She kept looking to grandma for a while. Her breath was going to stop due to the result of such statement. Grandpa was observing the situation while he was talking with his brother-in-law. Jolly moved to give a hug to grandma. Grandma shown it was the proper statement for her.
"if someone called me when was at my friend's house, people would tell them that I was at my friend's house. It is simple." Jolly told grandma while she was giving the hug to grandma.
"lets go to home" Jolly told grandma.
Grandma turned back to go home. At the stair, Jolly put her right hand over her grandma's shoulder and walked to the balcony.
"how could she live without us these 4 days. No mercy and no feeling for us. Oh my God. We were worried when she would come. It was hard to give our grandpa consolation. Every morning I just have to tell him only 3 more days! Only 2 more days!! Be patients!" Jolly said when she was walking with grandma. Still her right hand was over the shoulder of grandma when she was walking with grandma to showing her affection to grandma. Grandma twisted her face to show that she did not believe what Jolly was telling her. But she was not telling her anything.
"how could she have a such stony heart for us" Jolly added.

Jolly was giving grandma the tour to the apartment that in her absence everything was remains perfect while she was with her father's side relatives. After walked for a while, they came to the living room. A magazine was at the floor. Jolly took her hand off from grandma's shoulder and picked it up and put it in right place. Grandma gave a look to the whole living room. Grandma saw everything was OK. Everything was perfect. Everything was organized. Jolly was showing her the house and grandma was very interested to saw the house. The house was on orderly position. And grandma was giving the approval. It was kind of fun for Jolly. Jolly tried to understand what grandma was evaluating after see the living room. Jolly was looking at grandma's face to understand her evaluation. Jolly understood that she was satisfied to see the living room. Her eyes were still at her grandma's face. Grandma showed her satisfaction to see the living room. Jolly nodded her head with twisting her face that her grandma was satisfied to see the room was in perfect condition.

He Is My Mother's Father --☺ Anwar Al-Haqq

After that they went to the kitchen. An onion peel was at the floor. Jolly picked it up and put in the trash bag. Grandma also gave a look to the kitchen. Everything looked perfect. Jolly tried to understand her. Grandma was satisfied to see the kitchen. Jolly did same. Grandma found it also perfect. Then they gave a tour to store room. After complete the tour to whole house to let grandma to know that in her absence everything was fine, grandma and Jolly started to walk to my grandparents' bed room.

While grandma and Jolly were giving the tour of the house, grandpa was talking with his brother-in-law.
"Everyone in Kafrul Police Station was lived in panic when your nephew was at that office. Even the officer-in-charge was on panic while your nephew was there. I have a good connection to the Home minister. We promoted him to Police Station-in-charge at Tejgaon where my grandpa lives. I heard he is the source of terror at the Tejgaon Police Station. The Knee of the police at the Tejgaon Police Station started trembling after here the voice of your nephew." grandpa's brother-in-law said.
Grandpa was listening with great attention. It was sound good to him to listen his nephew's story.
Grandpa's brother-in-law looked at his watch.
"9.30. O! my God. I have to run to go to the office. I will call you from the office." grandpa's brother-in-law said and showed that he was in rush to go to his office.
Grandpa's said good-bye to his brother-in-law and came to his room. He took all his note books and calculator out. And put on his table as it was plane. He was calculating and looking at his note with great detail.

Grandma and Jolly came close to the door of grandpa after gave the tour the whole house. Jolly stood up. So was grandma. Jolly knocked the door.
"Grandpa! Can I come in" Jolly asked for grandpa's permission.
"Sure" grandpa said with affection.
Grandpa showed that his total concentration was on his work, calculate the rent. Grandma's temper went up to see the condition of the room. Jolly looked at her.
"O! Ho! How I could know that our grandpa is that messy" Jolly said to grandma.
"Look at the condition of the room" Jolly added.

Grandpa moved on from his chair and cough. It was not sound good to him that someone called him 'messy'. Jolly went to make the bed of the grandpa. Grandma still looked mad.
""Now she will start yelling to everyone. She will ask "did your grandpa miss any meal?"" Jolly said.
Grandma's temper went even higher.
""grandpa! Did I sat with you at the breakfast, lunch and dinner time, and asked you "grandpa do you need more rice, chicken, fish, meat, vegetable?" As long as you said No! No!! No!!! did I?" Jolly said.
Grandpa almost close his eyes and nodded his head to agree with Jolly. After see this, grandma's temper even went higher. Jolly stop to make the bed. She went out the room. After a while, she came back with a Weight Measuring Machine. She put it in the floor and went back to make the bed for the grandpa. She raised her head and pointed to the Weight Measuring Machine and said "grandpa! Would you please show her your weight?"
Grandpa was going to stand up from the chair to show his weight. But after saw the angry face of grandma which was toward him, he sat down again.
"you do not have to make the bed." grandma told Jolly loudly and angrily.
Jolly looked happy that she did not have to make the bed. She stop to make the bed. She was walking toward the door.
"I was in the heaven for last 4 days. Everyday I was calling me when I will come back to the hell" grandma told loudly and angrily.
Jolly went out of my grandparent's living room with smiling. My aunt saw her. After a while, my grandma cooled down. She smiled herself. Grandpa pretended that he did not see anything.
"Your grandsons Azim and Jamil gave you a hug before me"
Grandpa told grandma while his eyes were at his note and was calculating the rent. Grandma's temper went up again.
"you want to give me a hug in front of all your children, grandchildren and the people of the street. Do you think you will be able to find me alive after that?" grandma said to grandpa.
Grandma took the Weight Measuring Machine from the floor and went out of the room. Grandpa put back all his notes and calculator at his file cabinet. After that he went to the market to buy the grocery. Just after grandpa left the room my aunt give a look to the grandparents' room. She did not go inside the room.
"ho! if I knew that you and your grandpa had such a plan, I would

not come to made the bed for my father this morning." my aunt was talking herself while she was walking to her room.

Does Grandpa grown up as a violent Person? What does happen at the old age?

Next morning grandpa came from the market. He got the news that Azim was beaten by a boy of our neighbor. They boy's name was Nannu. It made our grandpa furious. I saw him first he sat at the chair and was thinking something. At the beginning he had the stony hard face. He looked very serious. After a while his face was becoming stony hard after that getting normal. It was going on for a while when he was sitting at the chair and was thinking deeply something. Finally he became a normal person but still he looked very serious. He took very seriously about Nannu beat Azim. He took Azim with him and walked to the door of that boy. Jamil followed them. Grandpa knocked the door very hard. No one answer. I went behind my grandpa. But I keep distance. I just went to give a backup to my grandpa. And I called four of my friends and told them to come to join with me. They were on their way. I told them that if I just give the hand sign such as when I would raise my hand up to start fighting with them. I also told them that if they find my or their other friends to bring them with them. As long as fight would not start, I would not let to know the Nannu's family that my friends came to help my grandpa. I told them to bring the hockey stick which usually gang member use to fight. It was easy to hold and at the same time hockey stick is very strong that it does not break down easily.
"Mr. Rahmat now is at the door. Now what would happen?" Nannu's father asked his wife with panic.
"Go and tell him that our Nannu beat him so what? Tell him that my brother is a Section Office at the Secretariat." Nannu's mother respond.
"he looked mad. I think it will not prevent him to attack me." Nannu's father told Nannu's mother.
"go tell him. My son beat your grandson. So what?" Nannu's mother said again.
"what do you mean 'so what?'" Nannu's father said.
"his brother-in-law is Deputy Police Commissioner. His nephew is in the Charge in Tejgaon Police Station. His grandson's mother

father was a Secretary, now his two sons are deputy Secretary and assistant secretary respectably and more. If he brings all of them, your brother will evaporated." Nannu's Father told with panic.
My grandpa again knocked the door hard.
"Mannu! Go and open the door for the Mr. Rahmat" Nannu's father told his other son.
"you! You put me in trouble" Nannu's father said while he was beating Nannu.
Mannu opened the door. He showed panic to see my grandpa.
"where is your father?" grandpa asked angrily Mannu.
"just talking with your father will not be enough." grandpa added.
Grandpa took the cell phone out from his pocket.
"I will call my nephew right not to arrest the whole family." grandpa said.
Nannu's parents hear that.
"his nephew will arrest us. Haa" Nannu's mother said in panic.
"go tell him. It was a mistake" Nannu's mother said and start beating Nannu.
"for you we are now in trouble" Nannu's mother said and beat him again.
"O! go and tell MR. Rahmat, it will not happen again" Nannu's mother told Nannu's father.
Nannu's father came to the door. He was in panic. My grandpa became furious.
"we are sorry for our son. I already punished him. If you want I will do it again. And it will not happen again. We are sorry" Nannu's father said in one breath. And he was sweating.
My grandpa little cooled down.
"I hope you will keep your word." grandpa said.
Grandpa put his hands to Azim shoulder and said "let go home".
Grandpa and Azim came home. Jamil followed them. Grandma gave a hug to Azim. And she cleaned his bruise. I was little surprise that grandpa forgive them that easily.

I knew that my grandpa is more family oriented person. He loved his grandkid like the other normal grandpa. Inside of him he is a kind of violent person as I know so far. He does not have physical strength to fight that is true. But he has the administration power to give hard time to an ordinary Bangladesh family such as Nanny's family. But I was surprise that Nannu's father just said sorry that was enough for him this time. At night I met with grandpa at the living

room. I said to him "after you hear that Nannu beat Azim you became furious. Nannu's father just told you that he was sorry. How come was it enough for you to cooled down?"
Grandpa looked at me and thought for a while and after that he said "after I hear that Nannu beat my grandson I was furious that was true. I was thinking to call my nephew and my brother-in-law and also to let to know the family members of Azim's mother. I was also going to call my nephew to arrest Nannu's family and to torture them at the Police station. And after that I would tell my nephew to send them to the jail. Even I would need to lie to make a strong case, I want to see that they should get the lesion. They need to get a lesion that they were messing around in a wrong place. Suddenly it was also coming in my mind the teaching of my religion "be nice to the neighbor and to be kind to them". My religion prevented me to behave arrogantly. At the same time it also was coming in my mind what our prophet (SAW) said "if you see anything is wrong, try to correct it". It was wrong Nanny to beat my grandson. My thinking to torture the family and at the same time to be kind to them were bargaining inside of my mind. At the same time I was asking God to guide me that I would be not one of the transgression and I would be not one of them who cross the boundary which their lord bestow upon them. After my desire arguing hard with the commandment of God, finally my desire gave up to the desire of God. Even it was coming in my mind that it would be OK to torture them and God would forgive even it would be considered as a sin. My mind also was saying it would be not sin. I came to conclusion it will be sin to torture them. And I will commit a sin which I already know that it will be sin. And it will be shame for me to ask God to forgive me for this sin. Finally, it came in my mind to just give them the warning this time. Peace is better than war. But only need to engage in war to correct the society when warning would fail. God is all powerful and all mightily. God knows very well what we reveal to people and what we hide from the people. And I cooled down. To God is the final return. Even it was difficult to see the bruise of my grandson, I back off to follow the command of my God. God told to follow his prophets. So follow the words of prophets are kind of following the command of God. Abraham, Noah, Jesus, Moses, Mohammed (PBUT) are prophets of God. I saw grandpa in sad mood "it was wrong for Nannu to beat his grandson." I put my hand in his back and give him the consolation and after that I went out from the living room. On my way out from the living room I tried to remembering what I

heard the stories of the prophets from my grandpa and how people gave them the hardship but they never disobey God. Therefore, God loved them and gave them highest status among the mankind. I was thinking "when people gave the hardship to the God's prophets and disrespect them, how God feels. I saw how my grandpa felt after his grandson was beaten by Nannu." I saw how somberly he said "it was wrong that Nannu beat my grandson".

Time to come back to the USA

It was 20th January. Day was Friday. I left Zia International Airport, Dhaka to come to the USA. All my family members came to say goodbye to me. Tear was at their eyes and they wished to see me soon.

My grandpa was a busy person all his life. And he is also a very social person. He used has a lots of friends. Now he does not have much to do except to collect the rent and to go to the market to buy the grocery. Azim, Jolly, Jamil, Lilly. Their school will open soon after a long vacation. Azam is very busy in his studying. The new school year would start. My siblings were very busy for their job and studying. Now Jolly have to fight like a bull to get admission at the Medical school for next 3 years. Need to study for day and night to fight for one of the seat out of 2200 seat with more the hundreds of thousand students like her brother Azam. He was studying day and night. No one would have that much time to spend with grandpa except my grandma. And some time his friends Mr. Ansari, Mr. Jalil and Mr. Matin and his other friends. Now the thought comes frequently to his mind for his nearness of death. Return to his lord. He always said " he does not have regret in his life about his achievement. He thanks to god to give him such a happy life. He does not have any complain about his life to his lord. His lord determined his destiny. And God determined the best things for him. He is not a superrich person in term of wealth, but he is a happy man. And tried to be a happy man.". According to the grandpa's belief "marriage is not just to live with someone happily in this temporary world but also to live with her forever in the hereafter." And I felt that what he said that he also showed those in his actions. After I got the US Student Visa, One day I was talking with him in the living room. After retired he became more devoted to God. I asked him "what made most of the people to devote to God after they retire?" He did not answer my question. He said "when I read at the newspaper that there have a billions of stars at the sky. And one star is like our sun. I see the power of God. I look at the sky. I tried to imagine the heaven. I see I am walking in a garden with your grandma where river flow. I think how the angel Gabriel brings the message from God to this world. One day my children would have the carrier which speed would be faster then the light and would come to visit their parents at the heaven. They would live in the heaven. And their heaven would be like the size of our earth or bigger. And they would live probably one second light year to thousands light years away from us. Or what ever. But they would be able to come to us in a very short period of time. Their carrier would make distance short between their heavens and our heaven." I saw him become emotional. Tear was in his eyes. I understood that this was not the answer of my question. This was his thought. He has the desire to live in the heaven with his wife. He is thinking of the nearness of his death. But he is helpless. He would leave behind his beloved wife and his children one day. And he wants to meet with them again. I was trying to remember his comment what he made one day "Now marriage become a rich man game for some rich in some part of the world. They do it to draw the people attention." My grandpa realized that it was sin to give bribe. And get loan on interest. He feels that with the sin he would go to the grave. I saw him how shameful he is to break the command of the God. And he asked God for forgiveness for his sin. This worldly matter does not impress him what was used to. He is probably to scare for his sin what he committed. And he scared to go to the hell. And he wants to correct it. But he also is not telling much to following the command of God. But family member realized it. I did not see anyone to cover their head at home. But they are doing it at home to keep my grandpa happy.

What we found inside of the mother's womb same thing is happening outside.

It was Saturday I came from Bangladesh to the USA. My class would start on Monday. A lot of thoughts were coming in my mind. Most of it was not a complete thoughts. When my class would started that could make my thought straight. I let to come all these thoughts to come inside of my mind. This time when I was in Bangladesh, most of the time I had nothing to do. One day my sister-in-law left a note on the table. I was reading her note out of curiosity. She wrote it to give a presentation to the Hospital where she works as a Gynecologist. The topic was about the reproductive system. I found it a very interesting article. Beginning of the note, she wrote about the anatomy of the female reproductive system. And she mark one, two, three to show how the sperm run to fertilized the female egg. First she show rhe sperm was at the Vagina, after that at the cervix of the uterus, then body of the uterus, then isthmus of the uterine (fallopian) tube, then ampulla of the uterine tube, then fimbria of the uterine tube which is next to the ovary where female eggs are produce. Fimbria has the finger like projection. She presented a nice diagram of the female reproductive system. It was like to me , if I tell a person to raise his or her both hands on his side about the 90 degree angle with their body at the side after that lazily bring the both hands 15 degree in the front. Middle of the chest could be compare as the Cervix of the uterus and the body of the uterus. Arm and the forearm as the Isthmas and the Ampula of the Uterine tube and the hand and the fingers of the hand is like the Fimbria. She wrote that ovulation occur 14 days prior to the menses. Example: if ovulation occur today, after 14 days menses would started. And she gave another example: if a woman has 30 days menses cycle, she would ovulate 17th days of the cycle or 14 days prior to the menses. During the ovulation, cervix has the watery secretion which helps sperm to run through it. But other time the section of the cervix become thick that sperm have hard time to run through the cervix. It was to me like a girl just keeps the gate open for the boy without saying any hi or hello. Girl attitude is like: if boy want, he can cross the gate which she kept open. During the ovulation, sperm has the opportunity to run through the cervix, from the cervix to the uterus, from the uterus uterine tube of the fimbria to meet with egg to fertilize it. It is like sperm run from the chest to hand to fertilized the egg. My interest to know about the reproductive system increased. Millions of the sperms participate in the race. Each sperm has a tail. Tail beat at the back of the sperm to move the sperm forward. Strong tail would give a strong beat. Sperm would have the rapid movement to the forward. Faulty, weak, handicapped, sick sperm would not able to travel to reach the fimbria. Tail plays the big role here to reach to the fimbria. Faulty tail would lose in the race. Tail is like the leg for the sperm. Estimated hundreds of the sperms would able to reach the fimbria. My interest to know about this sperm race went even higher. Very interesting thing was that the Ovary and the egg. Ovary is the organ where eggs are produce. Ovary threw the egg to the fimbria and fimbria catch it. Fimbria keep holding the egg for 12-24 hours without let it to go anywhere. These 12-24 hours, egg may wait for the sperm patiently. Egg has the earnest feeling to meet with the sperm. But do not want to move to meet with the sperm. If the egg can't meet with the sperm within 12-24 hours, egg may can't tolerated the overwhelm feeling which generated inside of them to meet with the sperm and die. If the egg meet with the sperm, egg feeling for the sperm disappear or keep in secret, and started for plotting the new game, and demanding that sperm should have the big shoulder and they are created to carry all the burden. Sperm carries the egg to the uterus from the Fimbria. It is kind of sperm to escort the egg to take to the uterus.

At the end my sister-in-law concluded her statement: *it is the duty of the sperm to run to meet with the Oocyte at the Fimbria (distal part of the oviduct) and after that sperm escort the egg to the uterus. On the way to the uterus, bond become strong between them (one cell →multiple cells) with the support of the environment. The whole process is the mutual understanding between the sperm and the Oocyte. Like if any of these has the defect like genetic disease, mutual understanding would fall apart. And miscarriage would occur. Escorting the girl does not only occur in the world, it also occur inside the womb of the mother. Nature determined "girl is special".*

I was thinking what could happen if the ovary forcefully thrush the egg and the egg reach the orifice of the cervix. In this case sperm would meet the egg at the orifice of the cervix, and probably outside the mother womb also could be different. A female does not have to let her heart to break into pieces with the feeling for the boy and her mouth would busted out with the words 'I love You' before the boy without any hesitation or scare to have the shame to say so. I mean girl would tell the boy first "I love you". Custom for the Man have to take the initiation to make a relationship with the girl would be abolish. Or such custom would never exist. I would see girls are waiting for the boys at their gates. And it would make my job easy to make a relationship with a girl.

Fimbria is like protecting the egg from the environment like the family members protect the female from the unwanted and hostile environment. If sperm could reach the fimbria, sperm would fertilize the egg. One sperm would win the race and would fertilize the egg. And it would shut all the door for other sperm that they can't enter into the egg to fertilized it even hundreds of sperm would reach to the fimbria. Strong sperm win the race. Fertilized egg with the sperm would turn into the Embryoblast after some days. And It is like Mrs. A throw a ball and Mrs. B catch the ball and keep holding the ball without passing it to anyone. Sperm fertilized the egg and would escort the egg by walking back to the uterus to implant it on there. If either the egg or the sperm has the genetic disease or environment of the uterus is not suitable, Embryoblast would die or baby would born with genetic disease or growth abnormality. It is like: there is need good relationship between father and mother and also the good environment to let a person to become something in their life such a successful businessman or doctor or lawyer etc. Problem in between father and father and bad environment could let a child to develop with psychiatric problem, or that child becomes an unwanted person in the society. So to develop a good baby inside the uterus is like to need a good family and good environment to raise someone as a good person. I found what we see in the outside world that same thing is happening inside of the mother. I also realized that my finding could not be very decisive about what I found inside of the mother and what I am experiencing in this world. This is the way nature could work. Creating the mystery surrounding its creation that we human being could not find always the decisive answer. People could raise a lot of question without find the answer. But people could realize 'the mighty' could be the perfect attribution for the Nature. And we the human being does not have capability to fully understand the Nature. My grandpa said "if a man wants to know the mystery of the woman, he would be exhausted". This mystery could work as a shield to protect the women. And keep boy on running to make the muscular muscle tired, and which could made the society harmonious. My grandpa also said that God created everything what have exist in this world. According to grandpa, God also created the womb of the mother. What is happening outside of the womb also created by God. But we do not fully understand of it. And we do not able to completely make relationship one to other. My grandpa said "there is no mistake and contradiction in the Koran. Whole book is logically approach to present it to the people. But in some point it did not tell everything about the information. Probably God thinks people do not need to know everything. So he kept holding the information to himself. God did not give the power to a human being to fully understand his knowledge and the mystery he created surrounding the human being. My grandpa gave the example. He said we human being would die just one time. There is no death at the hereafter. After destroy the whole world, God will let all his creation to taste the death which include also the angels. After that he will give the live to them again. How all of these will occur only God keeps the knowledge himself about it. What is going on in this universe we don't know. This is even beyond our imagination.

I was thing about my grandparents after read the note of my sister-in-law. How my grandpa was on run to propose to my grandma. I was tried to imagine how Moti grandpa lead a group of my grandpa's friend to run toward the house of my grandma's father on behalf of my grandpa and how the grandma's family tried to protect her. Even my grandma's pesky younger brother became the protector for her and created problem for my grandpa. But my grandpa was a determined person. And he overcome all the obstacles and finally win the race without competing with other person. Just he competed with the environment. When I was thinking about my grandma, I did not find any evidence that my grandma first time showed any interest to my grandpa. My grandpas went to my grandma's father house and marry her. After that he respectfully escorted her to his house. I was thinking: if the ovary throws the egg forcefully or ovary has the tail like sperm or wings and the egg wait for the sperm at the cervix of the uterus instead of the fimbria, how would it be like? Probably it would make the task of my grandpa to marry my grandma easy. My grandma would wait for my grandpa close to his house or at his house. Why did not the ovary throw the egg hard or egg does not have tail or wings? So the egg could reach to the cervix of the uterus. I was asking this question myself. What a natural selection for the girl! The egg waits at the Fimbria. Egg can't reach it destination, the uterus, without the help of the sperm. Probably natural has selected for the girl "girl need man touch to be flourish and to reach their destination" What a natural selection for the boy! Ovary throws the egg softly and fimbria just keeps it holding for 12-24 for the sperm to fertilize it. Keep boys on running. And I saw how my friends were in run. And story of the

sleepless night. When I was a ninth grade student and my mom saw that I was on run, she rebuffed me.
"if I see you to run behind a girl before you would finish your college degree, I would beat you with the bloom and I would drive you out from the home" my mom said.
"I would find a girl for you" my mom assured me.
"study hard. Throw out the girl from you mind" my mom added.
After I got rebuff from my mother, I stop to run to come close to a girl's house. Girl is beautiful. That was my reaction to a girl.

My Father's Father

My Father's Father

I was thinking about my paternal grandpa. He was a teacher of the religious study at the primary level. Thousands of teachers like him have in our society. Their job is to teach about God which frequently talked about to prevent the people from the sins. Bribery, deceiving other all these are considered as sin. But the moral values of the society are deteriorating. Bribe is considered as a gift. And poor farmer run away from his home because he failed to give back the money with interest what he borrowed in his hard time of his life. And his hard life even more aggravated. Rich are neglecting the poor. Powerful person are oppressing the weak. People are living with the false hope and the false promise. And falsehood becomes easy to promote then to remove it. If my paternal grandpa's was alive today and his teaching could appeal to the people and remove all the unjust rules from the society, I would write a biography for him. And I would need to find title for it. I would go back to the very beginning of his life. And I would title it: POWER OF A TAIL. It would be the appropriate appreciation for the tail which helped to bring a life in this world to strike to change the society for good. It helped the sperm to strike on an egg. And creation of a life had begun. Unfortunately he is not alive today. And I do not know much about him. Just a few stories of him I know about him from his brother-in-law. My grandpa often taught the villager about the teaching of our prophet and urges them stickily to follow it. And the following the teaching of our prophet "promises to be in the paradise".

Angry Disease

It was a month of July. It was the Monsoon season in Bangladesh. Most of the rural area in Noakhali was under the water. Cholera broke out. Let me tell you little bit about cholera. It is water borne disease. People become infected with the germ of cholera by drinking water contaminated with the human feces where usually the cholera germ could be found. People drink pond, canal and river water. People did their bathroom job in an open place and contaminated the water with the cholera germ. Monsoon season help it spread out the whole village, union or even in whole district. When cholera broken out, it effect sometime the entire village and killed a lot of people. The Villager gave it name 'Angry Disease'. They used to believe that God was mad to them and he was taking away the wicked soul and sometime good souls also taken away because they did not prevent to a soul to be wicked. So God become angry and God is taking away the good and bad soul indiscriminately. People have to make God happy. Village priest like my grandpa have to do something to make God happy. At the night time the village people gather in a place and have a lamp in their hand that is surrounded by glass to protect it from the wind to put it off. They count the number of people God took away for that day out of his unhappiness to that village people. After that the village priest has to lead a prayer for the peace of the soul for these dead people who died due to cholera. After that in a bare foot and muddy road, they started walking and started to remember the name of God loudly. They praise God such as some time they say loudly "Allah is Great". And they asked God frequently to forgive them. Someone even cry out loudly with repent and humiliate them in front of God for the sin they have committed. They have tear and runny nose which they often hide behind the towel. They cried for their sin and they think God was mad to them. This way they gave the circle the whole village for God to become happy again to this village people and this piece of land. These people are looking for God to favor them. After circle the village, these people hope sadly that God anger will subside. They often wipe out their tear with the towel. After finished their circling the village, they gather in the same place. No one was talking with each other and was not giving other the instruction what to do. Everyone in their own way was asking God to mercy on them and to forgive their sins. They cry out loudly.

No one was there to console them. Most of them hide their face behind the towel while they crying out loudly or silently. After crying for a while, one by one they left the place silently with sadness without let other to know about their departing from the place. One by one the villager left the place within 30-to-60 minutes. As a leader of the sad people group, my grandpa left at last and became the witness for the sad moment of the villagers. Finally he himself left the place sadly. This heightened 30-to-60 minutes of the somber moment for the villagers were to ask God to forgive their sins. And circling the village to proclaim the name of God loudly 'God is one' and to praise his that he is a merciful God. They villager did all of these to please the God.

The villagers thought that God was mad to them. I think probably God was not mad to them. Death is way of people to depart from this world and return to lord which they already know. God just did not unfold his knowledge to these village people because God wants step by step to unfold his knowledge to the mankind. Now people know that just not using the open space as a bath room and boiling the water before drinking it can prevent to infect from the germ of the cholera. Just not let the human feces to contaminate the water. Even infected with the germ, they just have to replace the fluid and electrolyte and germ would go away itself and they have to handle the cholera patients with special care that they themselves would not be infected with the germs. Now in the market they have saline package which cost only 10 cents probably. One-to-five dollar is enough to save one person life. Media also have great roll to save the life of the people from cholera which was not available at that time. If commercial saline bag is not available, media suggested them to put one fist size of brown sugar in a hot water with a pinch of table salt and after that cool down the mixture and let the cholera patient to drink it. Anyway even my grandpa lead a group of people to make God happy that did not work to save the life of my grandma. After two weeks of her departure from this world, he himself was infected with the germ of cholera and departed from this world. And people were blaming themselves to annoy God. God gave this angry disease to their village because they committed sin and disobey God. And the village people know that when people disobey God's command people would be in trouble.

Or it could be possible that God was mad to them because they poop in the water which people use to purify them to worship God. After hear the story if I would meet with my grandpa I would confront him "God probably mad to the village people because they poop in the water which people use to purify them to worship God". After confront my grandpa I would put my hand on his shoulder to console him and tell him "see! Nowadays People does not poop in the water and they drink boil water and they do not get the cholera. Even they get the cholera, if they give the fluid and electrolyte on time, people being cure. See! God just did not unfold his knowledge to you before." After I would tell this to my grandpa I would think that my grandpa would instantly understand I am smarter than him and he would give me a thanks to clarify the mystery of the 'Angry Disease' to him which they think that it was beyond their capacity to understand. It was beyond their capacity what God actually play with them by giving the 'Angry Disease'. This 'Angry Disease' could be the way someone to depart from this world. Or God gave this disease in their village to test them to see how this villager would react in time when disaster comes to them. God wants people to be patients in time when they experience distress. Good or bad time, people always have to be thankful to God. This is the God who proclaim "God determine people's destiny and every moment we pass in this earth we pass our time out of his mercy." But it was clear in their mind that without the permission of God bad or good can't happening to their life what God reveal to them in God's book Koran."

Or God knows the best why they had the cholera in their village and a lot of people lost their life due to it what the villager called 'Angry Disease'. They committed sins and God is mad to them and give this disease in their village out of anger or something else. Only God knows this very well. But I convince myself that God just did not unfold his knowledge to them about how to prevent and to treat the cholera which also God reveal to his book, Koran "God will reveal his knowledge to the people step by step".

Village Surgeon

My fraternal grandpa had a bald in his head and most of the time he use a Muslim cap to cover his bald. He pressed the cap hard that the cap can cover his whole head. Beside teach in a religion school, he was engage in taking care of the health of the village people. He also worked like a little surgeon at the village such as he did the circumcision to the boy and people from the neighboring village also come to him to get his service. The money he earned to teach in a religious school was not enough to run his family. He cut the foreskin of the penis of the boy. He did not use any anesthesia to do so. Someone have to hold the boy tightly that the boy can't move while he was doing the procedure. The boy was on sitting position and strong person hold his both legs tightly. Sometime he also needed additional help that the boy can't move. After take the foreskin out he put some white stuff which could be antibiotic in a thin piece of cloth and use it as a bandage.

After bandage the penis of the boy, grandpa gave the instruction of the parents not to let the boy to take shower for seven days. Just let the boy to washed the body with a wet cloth. In term of diet, he had forbidden the boy not to eat any fruit which has sour taste. It may cause the pus at the wound of the penis. Food such as fish curry or any curry should not have any water in it. It may cause the long time to heal the wound. Dry curry would help to dry the wound as my grandpas used to believe. Dried food was recommended. After seven days, he recommends the boy to go to the pond and sit down in the water for a while and let to separate the Band-Aid which becomes stick with the penis. Onetime one of his patients was sitting at the pond to separate the band aid from the penis. His hands were in his back to support him and he was looking at the sky. A duck was nearby and thought probably could be fish and hold the band aid inside the beck and full it forcefully which hurt the boy. Now grandpa gave them instruction after seven days, boy have to go to the fond with a stick in his right hand and drive out the duck that it can't come close to the band aid. After that sit down at the water and make a small wave over the band aid by left hand and it would slowly separate the Band-Aid from the penis. After that grandpa visit the boy and they cook good food for the grandpa. At that time he also give additional instruction, if it's were needed. All these services he offered to the people and he did not have any fixed rate. Whatever people can effort that they gave to the grandpa. When they gave the money, they bring the money to side pocket and he just grab the money and put the money in his pocket without counting it. He had to give a big smile to show the people that he was happy whatever the people offer him. Sometime people did not give any money and they gave coconut or a chicken whatever they produced or domesticated. Some poor people even don't pay any money. He put that on God's account. He said "God determine the people's destiny". My grandpa said in his words what God said to the people "don't scold the destiny. I am myself is your destiny." So grandpa show his smiley face even the poor people can't pay him any money. He believes strongly that God made these people poor. This is the reason these people can't offer him any money. But his duty is to admit it; and he should not show any discontent to these poor people, because they did not able to pay the money. He lent it to God and God would pay him in the hereafter. He thought this is the God who made this people poor. and did not able to pay him for the service he offered them. For this reason he did not show any discontent to the poor people. Because if he showed any discontent to the poor people, God would be mad to him and he may be deprive of the reward at the hereafter.

Office

My grandpa has small office at the village Bazar. Different people come for different reason. Just I am giving some example. One person believed that his son has poor memory and he could keep in memory after read the school text book. My grandpas hold the forehead tightly and read something and after that blow the breath to the boy's head. Sometime he wrote down something in a paper which also does not have any fixed rate to write it down for the people. But it should be inside a silver capsule which they have to pay. Blowing breath or writing in a paper something does not have fixed rate. Whatever people want they can pay. No payment that's ok too.

Jinni

My grandpa toughed the villager "what a Jinni is?". He said God not only created to human being to worship him and destine to go to the hell or the heaven, but he also created Jinni. Human being was created from the clay and Jinni was created from the 'fire'. He compare Jinni is like the oxygen which we can't see but we know the existence of it. Oxygen go inside of our body through the lung. Without it we would have mental trouble which my grandpa learn from a medical doctor who became self-taught priest with the help of a Mufti, Islamic scholar. Same way Jinni can go inside of our body. There is a bad Jinni and also has the good Jinn. Bad Jinni is like the Toxic substance. Cyanide, for example. It can harm the people by creating the bad thought into the brain. "All the evil things are happening in this world are inspired by the Jinn" Grandpa told to the people.

"Satan is belong to this group of God's creation. Satan is the head of all the Jinni who harm the people. Disciples of the Satan end of the day report to the Satan what they did? If a disciple of Satan reported that he inspired a person to murder another person, Satan replied that you did not do nothing. You did not able the break the relationship between the husband and the wife. You did not able the break the kinship. Satan is not satisfied with the worked of his disciples. And disciple of the Satan encourage to do even more harmful deed to the human being." Grandpa added.

"Those people who do harm other and do all the bad deed, these people also the disciple of the Satan." Grandpa said.

Sometime some people were captured by the Jinn. After the person was captured by the Jinn, whatever was coming out from the mouth of that person it was not his or her. Jinn is talking through his or her mouth. Often my grandpa was called to drive out the Jinn from that person's body. My grandpa visited the house of the Jinn captured person. First he read something. Request from the Jinn stated coming to be nice with him or her. My grandpa blew the breath to the Jinn over that body of the Jinn captured person. After that he take a bamboo stick and make a curve on it middle. Put small finger inside of it. My grandpa gave a hard squeeze over the finger and Jinn started saying he/she is leaving that person. Jinn run away and the Jinn captured person lost the sense for a while. And after that the Jinn captured person stated talking as a human being. On the way to home, Jinn could take the revenge to hurt my grandpa. So grandpa must have to carry a stick with him. When Jinn fight, it does not use any weapon. But when he sees there is a weapon is to a man's hand that let the Jinn to keep distance from that person. Jinns are stronger than human being. They have the physical strength to defect the human being but can't defect a man when that man carry a stick or weapon such as this weapon could be iron bar.

Treat Jaundice

One night my grandpa found the processing of treating the jaundice in his dream. He found someone told him to go to the garden where vine trees have. That person took him close to the vine tree and told him to make a wreath by using this vine tree. These vine trees have to cut into the small pieces and after that need to make a wreath. After that the wreath has to put on top of the head. The wreath has to slide down from the top of the head to the feet and on the way the wreath would take away the yellow color from that person's body and the jaundice would be cure. With these techniques he treated some people's jaundice. But for some people when he saw the jaundice is getting worse he recommended them to go to the Hospital. He told them God gave them the disease and God know when he will cure the disease. We only can put action to get cure from the disease. He believe the tree have the miracle power to cure the jaundice that was the reason he found this technique to cure the jaundice on his dream.

Anyway if my grandpa would alive today, he may have an office next to my brother's clinic. Even they would have argument how to treat a people with jaundice, after some point they would cooperate with each other. When my grandpa would fail to treat a person with jaundice, definitely he would recommend his patients to see my brother. When my brother would surrender and disease went out of control of the medical field and only thing would be sure that the patients is going to die soon like a patient with liver cirrhosis, my brother would call my grandpa again to become the spiritual healer. This patient day are just numbered that he is going to meet with his lord soon. The patients need my grandpa to perform some religious ritual for him and let the patients to read with him and ask God for the forgiveness. The patients would find the mental discomfort. He would get the assurance from my grandpa that probably his hereafter would be better than the life he has in this world. So my grandpa would advise him to be mindful of God. And ask God continuously to forgive his sin.

What did I think about my Grandpa?

After I hear all those stories about my paternal grandpa, I though it were probably part of the religion. Now I know that religion have nothing to do with it. It was my false idea that because he was a Muslim priest and all of his activities were run base on religious instruction. It was my false idea that whatever he did was part of the religion. If he had the highest degree in Islam religion probably he would not do something to feed him such that the technique to cure the jaundice. He did all of those jobs just to have a roof on top of his head and met the demand of his hungry stomach which would give him energy to walk over the land of God to go to the house of God, the mosque, where he lead prayer five times a day to fall in protraction over the land of God to glorify God. He asked the God to give him a Good life in the hereafter and also in this world. Without questioning God, he was readily to accept hunger, disease or whatever discomfort would come to him as a test from God. He used to believe that God would test him that did he is faithful and obedient servant to God or not? And at the same time he asked God to make the life easy for him and for his only son and for all the Muslims. And his son and his offspring could be the faithful servant of God.

He left little wealth in this world the time he departed from this world. He advice the people "earn money such a way what God gave you the permission to earn money. If you earn money in a way which God did not give you the permission, you commit a sin. When you will die you will leave behind this wealth, but you will take the sin with you which will be the cause of humiliation when you will meet with your God."

Anyway diarrhea cut short the life of my fraternal grandparents and cut short the career of the construction business of my maternal grandpa. My fraternal grandpa was a simple person. Simple disease like diarrhea which just need to replace the fluid and electrolyte on time to save the life of a person took the life of my grandpa. And he died in young age. He would never comeback to this earth. He departed to live permanently in the hereafter which he had the firm belief.

GRANDPA'S THOUGHT ABOUT DEATH

One day my grandpa was at his shop and was reading the newspaper. After I saw him, I entered to the shop. I sat next to him and he gave me few pages of the newspaper to read. I told him my conversation with Carol and Jenia. He just told me "anyone will make the task of other human being easy; Allah will also make his life easy."

"Whatever has in the heaven and this earth is belongs to God and God has the power over everything" he continue.

I saw he was talking like a philosopher, but his thoughts were not organized.

"God's reward is permanent. Anyone will help other human being to walk in the land of God to earn their living, Allah will reward them" grandpa added.

"one day this earth will vanish. Human race will vanish from this eath. But the reward of God will be permanent. There is no beginning or end for God; but for the human being there has the beginning but no endind. " he continue after took a pause.

My grandpas remain silent for a while after that he told me a story of his friends who fell in love to a girl. He said "we were standing on a bridge where underneath a big canal flow. We just finish our 10th grade board exam. My friend just saw the girl and fell in love to her. My friend said "it was a magic; and it was sweet and beautiful." He also was a career oriented person. The girl was seventh grade student at that time. She was going home in the evening with a group of girl after finish her school for that day.""

My grandpa said "my friend wrote a poem for her but I can't remember that whole poem now. He took a pause and recite two sentences from the poem " when you smile, precious than gem flow. When I look at your eyes, I feel to meet with you in the heaven again.""

"you friend wrote a poem too" I said with little surprise.

My grandpa gave me a hard look and started talking again "Girl was pretty. My friend proposed the girl after she finished her 10th grade board exam but did not get any respond about does she like him or not. Only she said to my friend to contact with her parents. He was a medical student and thought it was not the time for him to marry".

A deep breath came out from my grandpa and said "when my friend was in Dhaka and was a medical student, he got the message that his love one married someone else. Tear was drifted out from his eyes. He was on true love with that girl."

One of the friends of my grandpa's friend from medical college asked him "when you were in love with this girl, did you think to go with another girl even for one day and even your love one would never know it?"

"out of fear of rejection from this girl, I did not even look at any other girl. I had the thought she probably would know it and would reject me.. I was in process of learning what she like and what she does not like. I tried my best to keep away from it what she did not like" This was the respond of my grandpa's friend.

My grandpa become silent for a while and said "If we could see the God, we would probably fall in love to him instantly where we can't compare the human being with God. God is unique. There is no one like him. The difference between God and us is that he can create things and he has the power over everything. We need his help but he does not need anyone help."

He took a pause and continued "this bridge would become frail one day and would vanish, but this bridge is witnessing that one human being fell in love to other human being. Some of these loves would be permanent. They would meet with each other again in the heaven."

I asked myself "what does he mean?"

I was thinking myself "you children made a mistake to keep you at home. They should send back to your construction business. Now you have time to think about these old stories."

My grandpa become silent again and was thinking something deeply.

I looked at my grandpa and said with surprise "your friend just saw the girl and fell in love to her. Very surprise! Just see a boy, this girl even could have desire to bite the boy."

My grandpas became little annoyed and hide his face behind the newspaper.
"This girl is a normal girl" my grandpa said little angrily.
"This girl raised three of her children to be well educated person." My grandpa added.

After he brought my sister from her medical college with making a story that he was sick, he was thinking it was not good thing to do. It was a kind of deception and lie. He may commit sin. He did not prevent his temptation to meet with my future brother-in-law. He was talking about it with me and I saw there was a mental discomfort on him even we knew that he has asthma and sometime it get worse. He said "what I did was as example of living with someone by their own desire, but not to submit to the wish of God. I did not able to prevent my desire and did not submit myself to the will of God. As a Muslim, I can't deceive other and I can't lie to other". Our grandpa remained silent for a while and was saying something on his own silently. After that he released a big breath and told me "today people don't use the hijab in the name of modernism. If this is the definition of the modernism, people are following Satan." I gave a suspicious look at him.

"Islam does not prevent people to live in high tech society; Islam does not prevent them to give higher education to their daughter." He added and remained again silent for a while.

After remain silent for a while he said "my younger daughter is specialized in medicine. My first daughter is a professor in a college. Both of them use hijab out of fear of God. The knowledge they learned was from God. God gave them the ability to learn his knowledge. I am proud of my daughters that in the name of modernism they did not uncover themselves and challenge God. In the name of modernism some people are trying to disobey God and his prophet. But to God is the ultimate return and he will take the full reckoning."

After remained silent for a while grandpa said "The definition of modernism should be limited to the advancement of the knowledge of a society but should not include anything which could disobey God according to his guidance."

I saw at this stage of his life, he was scrutinized about his committing sins. The thought process of committing sin was going on in his mind. First I thought it may be the psychiatric problem. I talked with my brother about it. He said "this is the normal way to someone to deal with the reality, the imminent death. He was looking for the fault and at the same time he was correcting himself to purify him. If he was constantly just thinking about one sin and at the same time he was not trying to correct himself then we could assume that he may have the sign of mental problem. If someone jumps one subject to other constantly without giving any sense to their audience what he/she is trying to say also could be the sign of mental problem. But our grandpa stay with the topic until he finish the topic to give his audience the sense of understand what he was trying to say. So he does not have mental problem. My brother gave me the assurance with smile. He was seeking the God's guidance and at the same time he was judging his action that he was not violating the God guidance. People need high mental capability to do so, I mean someone needs higher level of brain function to do so: follow the guidance and at the same time judging the action base on the guidance that his action was not violating the God's guidance; this was show the personal integrity and a person with discipline. When he found a fault on his action which does not comply with the God's guidance, he was repenting and trying to correcting himself. A person with the psychiatric problem does not have such capacity."

"And his thinking about God and his sins will not make him a psychiatric patient" My brother gave me the assurance. "

My brother took a pause and said "Grandpa read Koran and the other Islam book to remove his all doubt that there is no God but Allah and Mohammed (SAW) is his messenger. What did you experience about the action he is doing is base of the guidance of the book of God. God's book helps him to build up such a faith. His faith is driving him behind to do all these actions. His faith is driving him to have a strong desire to go to the heaven. People need high level of intellectual capacity to understand books and find the evidence to build up such faith. Koran helps him to remove the doubt that indeed there is a God. "

My brother left after he told me that our grandpa does not have any mental problem. I was thinking myself that without know the psychiatric problems, we should not be suspicious about a person that he may have psychiatric problem. Even we think a person may have psychiatric problem, we should ask someone who have at least some knowledge what psychiatric problem is.

Azim thinks grandpa does not have anything to do other than to memorize the newspaper. After I talked with him, I understood that he was not memorizing the newspaper. Behind the newspaper, he was thinking about his death. And most of the time he talked with me about God, God's prophets, and his book, Koran. Anytime I tried to talk with him, he was trying to come to the topic about God. Initially I was thinking why he was talking with me more about the religion. In Bangladesh, people think the children of a Muslim could convert to some other religion or they would not practice their religion when they would live in a non-Muslim country. They would lose the spirit of the religion. My grandpa probably concern about my soul. By and by I was trying to be his good listener. After all, his daughter is my mother. I do not want to make her mad to me.

One day I was talking with him in the living room. He was reading the newspaper. While reading the newspaper, he said "if someone would have fear for God in this world, they would not have fear in the hereafter. If anyone wants to love God, they would seek the knowledge what are the commands God gave to the mankind to do to please him and what acts could raise his anger. Out of fear not to make him angry, they will refrain from doing so. This is the way people can show their love to their lord. People have no authority to invent something their own to please God when God himself gave the instruction what can please him. If anyone tries to invent something their own to please God, they are just over ruling the God command and God would reject them".
I shake my head to show him that I agreed with him. After that he changed the topic from fear of God to smoking and he said "smoking is a like someone is committing the suicide which is an unforgiving sin and will live forever at the hellfire as our Mosque Immam said but I don't know it. I was smoking when I was 16 years old. And I quit smoking when I was 45 years old because doctor told me that I could have lung problem if I continue smoking. After hear this, your grandma forced me to quit smoking."
Grandpa took a pause and was thinking something.
I was talking myself silently without let him to know "therefor, you have asthma now. I heard it too at the Friday sermon at the mosque. Probably you knew it to when you were 16, but you just did not pay attention to it".
Grandpa continue " smoking could shorten the lifespan. If it does, I have shorten my time to worship my lord"
He took a pause. I just wondering to know what did he wants to say. He continued again "better to ask the Immam about it".
"yea! You should check your status with consulting with Imman" I said.
Immam is kind of Pastor to the Mosque,
 Grandpa changed the topic and said "living up to the old age is blessing from God."
"Why are you saying this?" I asked grandpa.
He told me the story of his friend who died at age of 18. His sentences were often half finish. So far I understood, at that age he

did not have any understanding about the God and the relationship mankind has with the God. He just pray Friday prayer and to make his dad happy he pray morning prayer and recite Koran which is in Arabic and did not understand the meaning of it and he did not have any intention to know the meaning of it. I did not find the difference between him and me right now when he was 18 years old. He showed me that he became panic to die at that age and what he was doing at that age.
"Possibility for your friend to go to the heaven is very slim. You think" I said.
"Allah knows the best" he responded.
"To God is the final return. No escape" he added.
I found him his though process is completely dominated by the death. Death cornered him down. He has no way to come out from it. I felt little shame and I was talking myself "we need to let you to think about your death. Death will overtake us. Possibility for him to die before me is higher. You fulfill your responsibility to your family. This is the time for you to fulfill your responsibility to your lord."
I did not fully understand about God but my grandpa started changing it for me.
He advised me "don't be arrogant. Arrogant people are competing with God and their prayer will not be accepted. Indeed arrogant people are doing rivalry with God which is ridiculous".
I was listening what he was saying and sometime asked myself "what does he mean?"
"I was earning good money and some of my relatives had relatively powerful position in the society which made me felling that I am better than some people who does not have such position in the society. Now I feel I am the worse one among the creation of God." Grandpa said.
"How did you compete with God?" I asked.
Grandpa said "God is good. All praises are belongs to God. I was thinking that I was better than him! him!! Him!!!" Grandpa pointed his finger in three different directions. God is all wise, almighty, and all powerful and so on. He is the one who make someone rich and poor and someone wise and mentally retarded. And we should not think one person is above other person and behave arrogantly. These all are just for test. God test the human being. Whatever God gave to a person that person should be thankful to God and whatever the person asking for and did not get it should not

complain to God with discontent. People just should ask God sincerely what they want base on what God permit them to ask to him. God will probably give them their desirable things in this world or hereafter. All the prophets went through the tests after tests. But they did not complain to God even all the hardship came to them.
"Oh! I see" I said.
Grandpa took a pause and said with releasing big breath "inna-Allah-ha Ga-pu-rer Rahim."
Grandpa continued "whatever has in this earth and in the heaven is belong to God and God has power over everything".
Grandpa's this statement about God made to smile which made him to look at me suspiciously. I was saying myself ""now he understands about God at the end stage of his life. After understand all of these, why are you still claiming "my daughter" "my car" "my chair" "my building"?."
He said "there was a time I felt sad to leave my family. Now I do not have such feeling anymore. The day we born, we were destined to die one day. Someone would die before me or after me. To God is the final return. No escape! No where to escape!! That's it."
He became silent. And started talking again "I wish all my family members will go to the heaven and I will meet with them there. For me death is like crossing a screen which is separating one room to the other".
He became silent again. And started talking again "your grandma would raise my status in the heaven. Because of her, God would let me to live with her in a good quality of heaven than I deserve".
How that would happen I do not know. I saw him he became little emotional. And I did not ask him to know about it.

Another day I was talking with him. He said "giving bribe and taking bribe, both are forbidden in Islam. I learned it from the school text book when I was a ninth grade student."
He left a big breath and said "Satan promise the children of Adam (PBUH) to take to the hell fire. God gave the Satan the power to do so. Whatever is naïve is come from God and whatever wickedness come from Satan. Both make the people to laugh without knowing the significant of it"
I did not understand what he meant by that. I was going to ask question about it but his mood change and I become silent.
He became silent. After a while he shown he was little shame. After that he became little mad. He said in low voice "if I did not give the

bribe to the Engineer, he would not give me money for the project I finished even I would go to his office hundred times in one year".
I said myself "grandma did not give bribe to anyone. Does it raise her status to God?"
"did you committed sin with full knowledge that giving the bribe is sin?" I asked.
Grandpa nodded for approval.
"Does God forgive this sin?" I asked.
Grandpa said " in this case we have to humiliate ourselves in front of God. And show the God that we feel shame and we would not do this again."
After I hear it I talked with myself "yea! You are right! After your construction career is over, now you are saying you will not give the bribe again."
You did it. After a while I felt shame and remember what grandpa said "Whatever is naïve is come from God and whatever wickedness come from Satan. Both make the people to laugh without knowing the significant of it. My grandpa is telling me his sincere prayer to God and that made me almost going to laugh."
My grandpas remain silent for a while. And the words came out from his mouth " in-na-Allah-ha Ga-pu-rer Rahim. Which mean 'verily Allah is oft-forgiving and most-merciful' ".
I saw there was a feeling of guilty in his face and he was repenting for the sins he committed. The thought came in my mind "people are killing each other. People are committing crime and dying while they are committing crime. What will happen to them? These are the horrible sin as my grandpa told me. One time he told me "God is very severe in punishment." He probably has fear of God and he has fear of God's punishment. "God said that whoever will fear me in this world, they will not have fear at the hereafter" Grandpa told me God say so. "Unforgiveable sin is someone denied him as their lord and make a partnership with God" my grandpa told me.

My grandpa tried to come out from this emotional situation. He started talking "God want powerful one to save the week. Rich needs to take care the needy people. Protect the orphan and their property. Don't become rude to the orphan and to the family member. Take care the parents the way they take care them. Be nice to the neighbor. And fear God."
I became silent to hear it. Indeed you took care my father.

"Human being must have to make a love relationship with their lord to go to his heaven" he continued.
He became silent and was thinking something deeply.
He said "I did not know that giving the interest is kind of declaring war against God".
My grandpa became silent.
I knew that he borrowed money with interested from the Bank to finance to finish two of his buildings.
During the conversation he let me to understand that how come he can make a love relationship with God when in his life time he declared war against God. This interest business made his mentally discomfort.
"Allah said he will test the mankind" Grandpa said
"did you failed on the test" I asked.
Grandpa remain silent and after a while the words came out from his mouth "O-ya-tag-fi-ru-Allah. In-nna-la-ha Ga-pu-rer Rahim. Which mean 'seek forgiveness of Allah. Verily Allah is oft-forgiving. Most-merciful'. " [last verse of Surah Muzzammel]
To me he let me to understand that God left these two words in his book, Koran, as his love to the mankind "Allah is Ga-pu-rer Rahim." Otherwise my grandpa's hope to go to the heaven would evaporate. And all he could think that surely he would go to the hell.

"Mankind relationship with God should be like two lovers. They genuinely love each other. Let give an example. If one lover made a mistake and hurt other lover feeling, she/he should ask sincerely for forgiveness and need to correct himself or herself. And out of love other lover would forgive him or her. If an authoritative person love someone but that person deny that authoritative person and does not follow the command of that authoritative person and after disobey the authoritative person, if that person does not repent, it can raise the anger of that authoritative person and anger could raise up to certain stage that the authoritative would arrange the severe torment for that disobedient person. Same way God love to mankind will turn into to raise his anger and that person will taste the severe torment. So fear God and obey his commands. This is the way of the salvation." Grandpa said.
Grandpa remain silent for a while and said "God will punish his disobedient slaves who deny him. This is our duty to remind them about God and what God expect from the mankind to do for him."

"Following the guidance of God, Koran, will help people to establish a love relationship with God. Fear God and his punishment. God is severe in retribution. Ask God frequently for forgiveness." my grandpa added.

"Do you want to establish same kind of relationship with God?" I ask.

He remains silent for a while. He said "when you stand to offer Salah, you have to enjoy it and feel in your heart that you are offering Salah to please God."

I down my head and I thinking myself "so far I offer the Salah to make my dad happy and went to offer the Friday prayer to keep my name that I am a Muslim. Someone is not considered as a Muslim after missing four consecutive Friday prayers."

"We stand, prostate, bow down as our prophet (SAW) showed us to do to please the God. And in our heart, we are standing in front of God; and whatever we say in silent or loudly, God can hear it. We do it to please the God as a symbol to show our love to God as his obedient slave." He continued.

"We recite Koran during the Salah to praise the God. This is the book God reveal to our prophet (PBUH) to communicate with the mankind and to guide them how to come close to God. No one can add or subtract anything from this book. God will reject them if they do." he added. He compare the Salah is like a father is entertaining his little daughter by doing different gesture with his hands and body and saying something to praise the girl. But difference is God is all wise, all powerful and all knower." Grandpa said.

He strongly believes that no way human being wrote this book. Koran is a divine revelation. He suggested me to know the meaning of the Koran which could have lasting effect in my heart.

"I would try" I gave him the assurance.

Now he regretted what was forbidden in Islam such as listening music and others.

"Muslim means totally submit to the wish of God. Muslim does not live by their own desire, but they live with the will of God. They seek the knowledge to know what the commands are from God and they follow it without raise any questions." Grandpa said.

"A Muslim need totally submit to God to please God. This is the way a Muslim can show that they are in love with the God". He added.

My grandpa remained silent for a while. He continue "my wish about the last day of my life in this earth and before I will take my last breath are: after the offering of Salah in the month of Ramadan, in my heart I am as a slave of God is bowing with full submission to him and ask the God to forgive me all the sins and turn it to good deed. Allah is all powerful and all merciful and all forgiver. Hope Allah will give the guidance to all my offspring and the all the Muslims and the non-Muslims. Hope Allah will give me the last chance to praise him. And I would able to ask the God to die as a sin free man. Peace be upon to our prophet Hazrat Mohammed (SAW) and all the prophet who came to this world to give the guidance to the mankind." After he finish, I said Amin. Oh! Allah accepts the prayer of my grandpa.

We remain silent for a while and he continue "Last day of this earth would be joyous day for me like a lover is going to meet with his love one after a long waiting. I am going to meet with my lord." "surely it would be joyous day for you. There is no need to be sad and there is no need to shed the tears for you. Surely we also will meet with our lord soon. We will give you farewell for a short period of time with a good faith that you were able to perform your duty to your lord which your lord bestow upon you. There is no need to be sad for your departure from this world. God decided for you to come to this world and God decided for you to depart from this world. We can't show our discontent to the God's decision by asking God why he takes you away from us" I said with affection.

I saw the satisfaction in his face after he heard my respond and he said "before I depart from this world I would forgive all the mankind who did the injustice to me that because of me God would not keep holding to and not let them to go to the heaven with a hope that God also will forgive me". After he said that he hide his face behind the newspaper.

My grandpa is enjoying his life in this world. But at the same time he does not forget his duty to his lord. And also to his relatives who passed away. He visited their grave to pray for them and he pray for the peace for the soul of his relative after offering every Salah (five time daily prayer) and he donate money that Allah could give the peace of the souls of his deceased relatives. Like my father, after offering Salah I saw my grandpa to raise his hands to God and sound came out from his mouth "Ra-bir Ham Hu-ma ca-ma ra-ba-yani sogera". The meaning of this Arabic is "hey lord the way my parents take care me please take care them same way". Someone also translate it like this "Oh Lord! The love you created inside of them for me, create the same love inside of you for them".

As he is getting older, his love to this world is loosening and his thinking about God and his deceases relative becomes more frequent. He can't escape anywhere to avoid the meeting with God. And he will meet with his God like his deceases relatives. No escape. Now his only desire is to go to the heaven which is a beautiful place to live where he would have desire and his desire will be fulfill. At the heaven he would have a house which would be built with gold and silver. A lot of servants will be surrounding him to serve for him. My grandpa want to live with his wife happily forever in the heaven which will be a permanent place for him. Bird will be fly over and he will have desire to eat it. The bird will be roasted and will be present to him but no need to go to the bathroom. Therefore, now a day grandpa frequently says "this would is nothing but delusion and hereafter will be the permanent." He wants to live happily permanently at the heaven.

I Left behind My Family Again.

I went to Bangladesh from the USA, a marriage age adult. And most of the time I sat down at home with dry mouth. And I did not find any girl to knock our door to show their interest for me. I would be an Engineer after two and a half years. I heard that bridegroom with the Engineering degree have big demand in our society. I am 5ft 10 inch tall. I told my friends, relatives and the neighbors that I could run 5 miles in 50 minutes without taking any rest. When I stand with other Bangladeshi man, my head most of the time stay above the average head. I am also considered as a gentle man in my society. But I failed to get any attention and no knock at my door. And I was not on run behind a girl, because I need to follow the command of my mother. I was thinking: if the egg would come close to the cervix of the uterus, the result of it would make something different for my life. I would be the person to accept or deny the proposal in a respectful way. After I would be an Engineer, I hope my mother would withdraw her restriction and I would look for a girl. But I am worried: if I propose and girl would deny me, how much shame it would bring for me. Or I would like a girl but I would not approach the girl with the fear of denial. Sometime I think, nature really put a big task on the shoulder of the boy. I and my friends are the example of it. I was witness of a proposal of my friend. The Ha-ha, hee-hee sound of the girl spread out to the far distance where it was originated. And after that while he walked at the street, it made harder for my friend to keep his head straight. He usually laughs out loud. And when people asked about it, he put restriction on his face to express his smile and no sound came out from his mouth and no full face expression of smile. And people were seeking to get pleasure from my friend's this situation.

Probably in my absence mind I was thinking to protect me from the shame and also at the same time I was trying to console me by finding the Male supremacy to get the self-satisfaction. Probably I was scared to be shamed. At the same time I was looking to meet my inner demand, feeling to have a girl in my life. I was looking something against the proverb has about the girl in Bangladesh "girl chest would be to the point of busting to be piece by piece for the feeling of the boy, but their mouth would not burst to say to her love one "I love you"" I was looking girl's mouth to be busted and the word 'love' to reach into my ears. And also my environment encages me and did not let to bring out my feeling for a girl. All of these are the product of a absence mind. And the thoughts were not organized. There is no girl presence in my mind. Probably this was behind for all these thoughts process were going on in my absent mind. My grandpa taught me to live in the real life. So I do not have any imaginary girl. Even the imagination come about a girl in my mind, I learned to block it. Probably I was looking to blame someone for my this situation. And I found 'birth process'. I was blaming the ovary why it did not threw hard the egg or gave a tail or wings to the egg. I was looking someone to blame which one is more tolerable. Which one would not respond me back. I am losing the tolerance to make argument with the people. I said "all these occur in my life because of you and I do not want to hear you to deny it". After came from Bangladesh, I realized that I also gain 7/8 lbs. I was disappointed to discover it. Bangladeshi people are also getting health conscious. So they girls are.

Next morning after I thought about Bangladesh, I was little frustrated. In my mind there is a girl who I like when I was a ninth grade student. But I did not find the opportunity to tell her. I do not know "did she understand about my feeling for her?" She may go away by holding with someone else hand. Also I am thinking that I

am gaining weight. First I planned not to eat anything at the breakfast to lose weight and go for the jogging. But I change my mind to just eat 2 slices of bread with the peanut butter and the strawberry jelly. After I eat 2 slices of bread, I ate another 2 slices of bread. After that I become mad to me. I had a plan to lose weight. Now I ate 4 slices of bread. I was sitting at the kitchen with the frustration. My housemate came to the kitchen and saw me sitting with little devastation.
"are you 'OK'?" my housemate asked me.
"I had a plan only to eat 2 slices of bread, but ate 4" I respond.
"don't double the portion" my housemate gave me advice and left kitchen.
I sat at the kitchen for a while. I need to prepare for next semester. Most of the time I also come to the conclusion "what my mother did, did for the best for me." I am still studying. But some of my friends after 12th grade education, they lost their interesting in studying. They had more freedom at their home then me. And few of them were over controlled by their parents. I was thinking good think about my mother. Now she has one granddaughter. And at home, her time spent most of the time with her granddaughter. When I saw how my mother was spending her time with her granddaughter that also tell me how my grandparents treated me.

When my niece was seven/eight months old, she tried to stand up by holding my mother. She hold my mother's hairs. I saw my mother was trying to take the revenge by pulling her hair. But her head was shaved. In Bangladesh, people shaved the kids head with the hope that they could have well grown hair when they would grow up. Next day my mother put a piece of a cloth at the corridor. I was sitting with my grandpa at the balcony. He was reading the newspaper. My niece crawled and came to that piece of the cloth and sat on that cloth.
"hay! Hay!! Don't sit here. Don't sit here" My mother yelling to her. My niece crawled out from that piece of the cloth. It seemed to me she became little scared to my mother. She did not understood "what crime did she committed?". My grandpa was smiling behind the newspaper. I did not know the reason. Probably now also his daughter become the grandma. My mother yelling to us and there was a reason behind it. Now my mother is yelling to someone without any reason. After by niece born, we hear more frequently that my mother is yelling to someone. Now frequently we hear that

my mother are yelling to my niece.

Another day my mother was sitting at the floor of the balcony. My niece was probably 14 to 16 months old. My niece and her mother were coming toward the balcony. Someone left 3 pickle bottle at the balcony to warm it up because it was a sunny day. My niece went to play with that pickle bottles.
"don't touch it. Don't touch it." my mother yelling to my niece.
While my mother was yelling to her, it was shown that she become little scared. After a while she was dancing with little pleasure. Probably she was able to bother her grandma. My sister-in-law said with affection "yea! It is pleasure to be scolded by the grandma".

This time I went in Bangladesh. I, my mother, my sister-in-law, my niece, and my grandparents were sitting at our living room. My mother tried to organized one of the sofa. My niece was preventing her to do it. She sat at the sofa.
"move" my mother said loudly to my niece.
My niece even sat firmly at the sofa.
"as you growing older, you are becoming a troublesome for me" my mother said.
I jumped up from the sofa and went to close to my niece.
"you. You are giving trouble to my mother. How dare are you?" I told my niece by pointing my finger to her. As a younger son of my mother, I needed to punish someone who would become a troublesome to my mother.
"come here. Hold your ears and standing up and sitting down alternatively for 25 time" I ordered my niece by pointing to the floor of the living room.
"where does she get courage to bother my mother?"
"it is my duty to punish someone who would bother my mother" I added.
My niece went to my mother. And my mother hold my niece on her arms.
"you don't have to punish her" my mother told loudly with rebuff.
I become little bewilder. I went to the sofa and sat the place where I was sited with my sister-in-law and my grandparents were sitting down. I felt little embarrass. My grandparents and my sister-in-law were smiling at me. There was sympathy in their eyes for me. Mom!

He Is My Mother's Father -- ☺ Anwar Al-Haqq

You were always a loving and caring person. I missed my family while I was living at the USA.

Sometime I also thinking what would happen after class would start. In the first day of the class, probably there would be no class for me to attend. I would go to the cafeteria to eat food and probably I would see a beautiful girl sit down in front of me and her beautify would impress me. I would fall in love to her. Impressive! I would experience what is love. And at old age I would have the desire to see my lord. And I want to fall in love to him. Surely just a glance to my lord will be enough to fall in love to him. After I thought to meet a beautiful girl at the cafeteria, it came in my mind that God said "lower your gaze when you would see a girl". So I gave up my desire looking at a beautiful girl because at the same time it was coming in my mind what God said "follow the command of the parents as long as it will not go against God". I left it to my mother to find a girl for me to marry. After all I would not able to tell my mother "I would be not like your father." My mother sent me to the USA to be an Engineer. And I should be Engineer first, and I should not look for a girl to marry at this moment. Grandpa taught me what God said about how to treat the parents and at the same time he taught me that parents also should not be harsh to their children. Parents should not gave them the load which they would not able to carry. God said that he did not gave the load to the mankind which they will not able to carry.

Constantly all the memories of Bangladesh were coming in my mind. When last day's wishes of my grandpa come in my mind, I instantly respond "Amin". Oh! Allah responds to my prayer.

Sometime I just want to know about my grandpa. And how much influence he has in my life. I would ask Moti grandpa more about my grandpa. Probably my grandpa was like me when he was at my age. He was thinking about girl, career, and future like me. Like me he was thinking all these worldly matter when he was in my age. And like him I would be old one day. And I would find nowhere to escape to avoid meeting with my lord. And I would be mindful with the God. And I would appreciate God to let me to live to the old age. And I would have the same wish as my grandpa. I am a slave of God and I am going to meet with my master. And it would be joyful day of my life. And my wife would be the proper complain with me in the paradise where she would live with me forever. And we would never be old in the paradise. I would live this world with only desire "I want to live in the paradise and I want to work for it." Like my grandpa I would have strong desire to live in the heaven and I would find that this world is nothing but delusion and hereafter will be permanent place for us to live. And I would take every step to prevent me from committing sin and ask God frequently to forgive me and mercy on me and let me to work to go to the Paradise. I know this would be hard job to follow the all the commands of the God. Even I do not know very well of all the commands of the God. Even my grandpa also does not know all of the God's command very well and he himself sometime does something which is not allowed in Islam, I feel I just need to remind him about it to him to correct himself. And he is ready to correct himself due to the strong desire he has to go to the paradise like him grandson Azam who has a strong desire to be a medical doctor and are studying day and night to get admission in the medical school. He almost gave up his social life until he would not get the admission in the medical school. He is not living with his own desire to have fun and engage in entertainment activity which he usually like to do, but he is trying to comply with the Medical School Admission Committee to get admission in the medical school. Sometime I feel people lost the sense of what is sin and what is not. Even some acts are considered as a sin, but people are doing it. It seemed to be that the people lost the sense that it is a sin. For example, Hijab, taking bribe etc. I think it is the Satan who makes the change the society to accept it as not a sin what was used to consider as a sin. My grandpa probably sometime also loses the sense that it was sin and he did it. I just need to remind him about it. I am confident that he would refrain from doing the sin if I would explain to him. Because the strong desire he has in his mind to go to the heaven would refrain him from committing any sin in the future even it would cost him all his fortune. He is ready to follow the command of God. This is the God who has sole authority to let someone to go to the heaven. My grandpa understood it long ago.

"Paradise is the beautiful place to live with happiness forever" my grandpa told me. And he gave me advice "don't just rely on the Mosque's priest words. Always look at the source such as Koran and Hadith to find the authenticity. A lot of previous nations were misled by their priests by creating religion by themselves. And God himself rejected their created religion. God does not like people to create something their own to worship God when God himself gave the guidance to the mankind how to worship God. God rejected those people who put pen over the God words and thinking that God words are not enough for them and they need to invent something their own to satisfy God. This is a serious sin and this is an act of arrogant behavior."

After took a pause grandpa said "always respect those people who hold the knowledge of God such as like the Islamic scholars. Ask them questions and expect that they would answer your question best of their knowledge and their answer would be like you ask a question to our prophet (SAW). After get the answer, look for the authenticity of their answer. If you find any inconsistency in their answer, ask another scholar. If you find any inconsistency at the answer to any of the scholar, don't hesitant to ask more question and raise the question about the authenticity of their answer. If we don't do it, one day these groups of scholar would start selling the ticket to the heaven to the people with the inspiration of the Satan. But only God kept the knowledge about who will go the hell and who will go to the heaven like God kept the knowledge about the last hours, dooms day. Some people declared that such and such time, this world will be destroyed. But the hour came, we the human being still eat water and drink food. It was crazy that some people gave up their livelihood because of these people who mislead them. And these people were humiliated by their people for giving the false prediction which they have no knowledge. Same way those who would sale the ticket for the heaven to other people will be humiliated in the hereafter to deceive the people which is considered as a serious sin. This is also an act of arrogant behaviors. This people are competing with God."

The knowledge of my grandpa has about the religion, sometime impress me. His interpretation about the religion sometime surprised me. One day grandpa admit " If one day I would go to the heaven and I would be able to find myself that I am a better Muslim, it would be not just your grandma but it would be also Mr. Ansari who help me to be a better Muslim. Jesus, Muses (PBUT) were Muslim. A lot of time I did not understand the meaning of the Koran. It was the Ansari who interpret the Koran and Hadith for me and I was impressed by his interpretation about the Koran and Hadith. I asked the Islamic scholar to confirm his interpretation about the religion. When I first meet with Mr. Ansari he was nice to me. After a few months he started annoying me by poke on me the way he still does it to me. At first I felt to punch at his nose to make it flat. After I get the knowledge about the religion from him and he started impress me by his interpretation about the Koran and the hadith, his act did not annoy me anymore.

"Paradise is the beautiful place to live with happiness forever" my grandpa told me. My knowledge about the description of the heaven was limited with this one sentence. My final week before departed from Bangladesh, my grandpa mostly of the time tried to tell me what heaven is.
"It is not the accumulation of wealth or good position or higher university degree define the ultimate success. According to God, those who would go to the heaven would be the successful one." My grandpa told me.
"God wants people to ask God to let them to live happily in this world and in the hereafter. If you earn the true knowledge in this world, that will help you to understand the God even better. This is the reason probably our prophet urged both man and woman to learn knowledge even they need to go to a foreign country. This could be any knowledge and must have to be true. Earning knowledge could help people to understand not only the power of God but also to understand the mystery of his creation even we will not be able to understand every things of it." Grandpa continue.

Imaginary Heaven

It was Friday evening. Last Friday for me before I would depart from Bangladesh to come to the USA. After the sun set, my grandpa pray his Magrib prayer at the Mosque and came back to his store. He was sitting down himself and reading the newspaper. I was on my way to meet with my friends. We had a plan to play the badminton under the floodlights. I gave a look at his store. My grandpa saw me and I went to him. He told me to sit down.
"what is the date for you to go to the USA?" My grandpa ask me. I told him the date. He already ask me the same question 3 times before.
"Did you remember what was the sermon priest gave in the Friday prayer?" grandpa ask me.

"probably hell and heaven" I respond.
" you are right. He just tried to remind people about the ultimate destination of the people. He did not had time to describe what people would do in the heaven." My grandpa told me.
"Size of the heaven would be bigger than our earth for some people. Man and woman would never be old. They would be look very beautiful. Husband and wife would spend years after years just looking at each other. They would have desire and it would be fulfill. They would have desire to see their state and they would be there to see it. Heaven is a beautiful place to live where river would flow underneath of it. Gardens with tree and flowers. Bird would fly over. They would have desire to eat it. And bird would be roasted and let them to eat it. This food would not make them any urge to go to the bathroom. There would have servants to serve the food. Wine would be given which would not cause the toxicity. Food would be very tasteful." My grandpa told me. When he was telling me he was becoming emotional. His eyes become watery. I put my hand on his back to console him. After that I asked him to give me permission to go to meet with my friends. He knew that I would play badminton with my friend in the evening. He gave me permission to go to meet with my friends.
I was on my way to meet with my friends. It was a night of full moon. I looked at the moon. I tried to think about heaven while I was looking at it. I knew that moon has the mountain. I tried to image that my grandparents are on top of the mountain. After that they have the desire to sit in a place where a beautiful garden have and underneath of it a river was flowing. I was comparing it with a bridge which is over a river and the bridge has beautiful garden. My grandparents are staring at each other. After a while they see birds are flying over them and they has the desire to eat those birds. Birds are roasted and is given to them to eat it. Grandpa finds it very tasteful. He wants to eat the whole bird. Grandma first advise him to eat quarter of it to keep his blood cholesterol low and also not to gain the body weight. When grandpa eats the quarter of the bird, grandma insisted that grandpa should stop eating. And at the same time grandma has desire to eat the fruits. Fruits are presented to them. Now grandpa insisted that servants should clean the fruits thoroughly with the boiling hot water. I was looking at the moon while I was walking to meet with my friends. When my girl tried to enter on my imaginary paradise of my grandparent, I became emotional. I continued walking with watching the full moon and tried

to imagine it as the size of the paradise. My friend Abdulla which mean Slave of Allah was also on his way to meet with my other friends to play the badminton.

"What are you looking at the moon with that good attention?" Slave of Allah asked me with curiosity.

"On the moon where rivers are flowing under the bridges and on top of the bridge there has beautiful gardens." I respond.

"You mean moon has water" Slave of Allah ask me with surprise. He seemed to confuse with my answering to his question. I did not realized that my imaginations were flying over the moon. I just use the moon to guess what a heaven is.

"How many fingers am I showing to you?" Slave of Allah asked me.

"Three" I respond. His question grounded me on the earth.

Even I responded his question correctly, it did not convince him. But I did not feel to talk about my grandpa and his wishes with him. And I myself also was little emotional at that time. My imaginations were flying over the moon which I found more close to our earth to uplift my imaginations above it. I see stars as a small particle but in reality bigger than moon and sun as sign of hell.

"Biplop died in heart attack due to addiction to cocaine and heroin. He also had the hallucinations." Slave of Allah told me.

"I feel sorry for Biplop" I said. But what my grandpa told me was in my mind.

"We spend most of the time looking at the ground. We do not look at the sky and tried to understand the example God set up for us to understand how powerful he is. God just said 'be' and all these were created. Billions of stars" I said to Abdullah let him know that I was researching about the creation of this universe by God and I was trying understand the power of God. My statement did not convince him much. Still he was on puzzle "I found water on the moon while I was walking over the earth." Our conversation come to end when we both met with our other friends. That's help me not to create even more story to cover up my original imagination about the heavenly life of my grandparents and let Abdulla to know that I do not have hallucination. Now I realized I should tell him the truth what I was actually thinking.

Anyway I was thinking about the life my grandparents would have in the heaven on my way to meet with my friends. And at the same time I understood that what I was thinking about the heavenly life probably would not be 100% true. It is just my own creation of the heavenly life which I took base on my observation in this worldly life and the little description I learn about the heavenly life from my grandpa that day. Finally, I wish the desire of my grandpa would come as true "he want to live forever with my grandma in the heaven and he want to be among those who would be consider as a successful one".

--------------00--------------------------

This book is dedication with a prayer for the all the departed souls and for the people who are living in this world and submitted their will to none but only to God from the time of Adam (Peace Be Upon Him) until today. May God forgive their all the sins and save them from the punishment from the grave and from the hell fire. May God let them to live in the paradise? May God forgive the sins of my parents and my grand-parents and save them from the punishment at the grave and at the hell. May God let them to live in the paradise, the most desirable place to live?

=====================oo=====================
====

Mohammed Rahmat Ullah and other characters in this book are the imaginary characters which are based on the Bangladeshi people.

---oo-------------

I am looking for a traditional publisher (not a self-publisher) to publish this book. If anyone interested to publish this book or can help me to publish this book, please contact with me.
Anwar Al-Haqq
E-mail: noakhali92@yahoo.com

Write down your comment about this book

If I would be able to publish the book, 'He Is

My Mother's Father', my next project would be MASJID ....

www.ingramcontent.com/pod-product-compliance
Lightning Source LLC
Chambersburg PA
CBHW051702170526
45167CB00002B/509